Climbing Plants

Flowers & Plants

MAGNA BOOKS

Contents

Index

Introduction

Creating a structure in the garden

Climbing plants are often given a conspicuous place in the garden, and can have a strong influence on its overall appearance. They have long, usually flexible herbaceous or woody stems, which in nature climb up neighbouring taller plants, trees, stones or rocks, either attaching themselves or twining round them.

Most of these plants come from tropical forests in Africa and South America, while others grow in woodlands and scrubby slopes in subtropical regions of North America, South-East Asia and in some cases the Mediterranean. Many climbing plants have twining stems which wrap themselves round a support. Others, such as *Hedera* and *Parthenocissus*, are self-clinging; some, such as *Lathyrus* and *Vitis*, have tendrils. Some plants, such as *Clematis* and *Tropaeolum*, have twining leaf stalks, and others have to be tied in to create the desired shape.

Fruit trees have also been trained against walls in northern Europe since the late middle ages. Walls, particularly south-facing ones, create considerably warmer conditions than those of free-standing trees. Fruit trees, cane fruits and other supported plants can also be grown over a pergola or arbour. Apart from the plants described in this book, there are obviously many other trees and plants which lend themselves to being trained; these include many different trees, such as lime, holly, plane and hornbeam, though these require regular heavy pruning to keep them in shape.

Climbers and ramblers can add a great deal to a garden: they do need a certain amount of maintenance, but will definitely repay the effort.

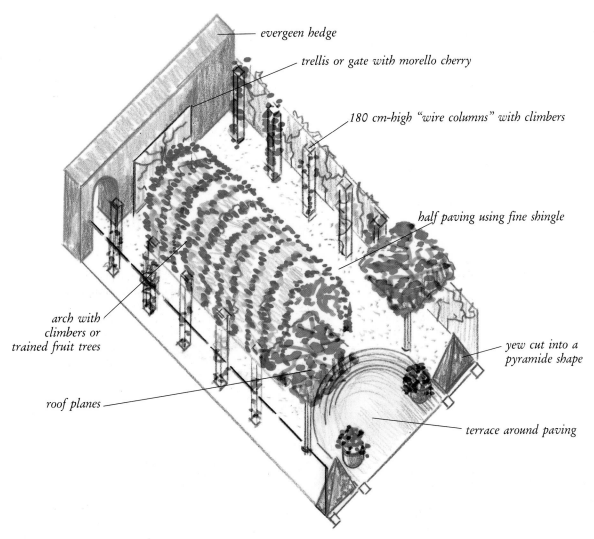

evergeen hedge

trellis or gate with morello cherry

180 cm-high "wire columns" with climbers

half paving using fine shingle

arch with climbers or trained fruit trees

yew cut into a pyramide shape

roof planes

terrace around paving

The design

Plan

A garden dominated by climbing and trailingplants takes patience and a willingness to prune regularly. However it also gives you a great deal of say both in where the plants go and how they are grown. But these are high-maintenance plants, and require a certain amount of long-term planning; if you are expecting to move home in the next few years, it might be a better idea to grow them in pots and tubs so that you can move them easily when the time comes. If you start pruning and training them now, the result in about five years' time will be very eye-catching. The plants will need more rigorous pruning than if they are grown in open ground, as their ability to root is limited.

This design centres on the pergola or arbour: a double row of pear trees which have been pruned to form a hedge. It needs an eye-catcher in the background, perhaps an ornament, a bench, a morello cherry (*Prunus* "Morel") trained on a trellis or one or more pots containing a pruned *Buxus* or *Taxus*.

Climbers and ramblers have also been grown along the hedge, with uprights just in front of it (buried at least 60 cm deep) joined by wires onto which the plants are trained. These can then grow away to their hearts' content, but can also be kept under control. This kind of structure will give rapid results.

Nearer the house, there are a number of trees and shrubs which have been carefully pruned and trained. The plane trees on either side of the round patio are fairly fast-growing and can be made into a roof if properly pruned and trained. This involves deciding the height at which you want to allow each tree to branch out; the crown may vary in height and be allowed to spread or limited in size, depending on how much shade you need. If you do not keep up the pruning, you will soon have a very substantial tree!

The space next to the patio is occupied by trimmed or pruned low *Taxus* hedges. What shape you prune them into is up to you: you might want to use wire structures to create geometric topiary forms such as pyramids, obelisks or balls, or animal figures; these will need annual clipping to shape.

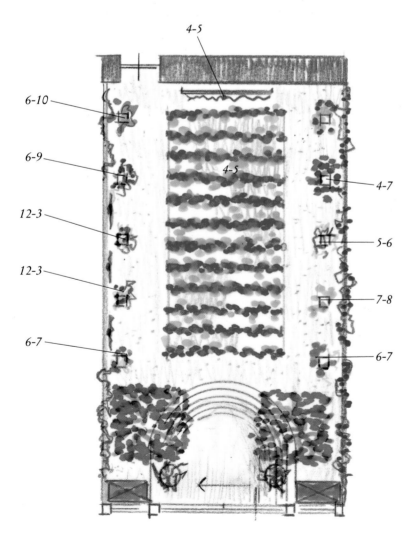

Month of the flowering period

Planting plan

There are several basic forms which have traditionally been used to prune and train fruit trees. Some of these are not easy and are rather labour-intensive, and so may require specialist help.

Espaliers have a central stem and pairs of branches trained horizontally along wires. In a *fan*, the branches are trained outwards in a fan shape. A *pyramid* involves pruning the bush in the shape of a flat Christmas tree, with the lower branches left long and trained outwards, and cut shorter towards the top. *Cordon*-grown bushes are planted at an angle of about 45° with the branches pruned to create a regular criss-cross pattern with the wires.

The pergola shown here is about 3 metres wide and 6 metres long; the pear trees can be trained along flexible tonkin canes if necessary. These are pruned into a hedge shape by removing branches growing towards the front and back, and trained round into a dome at the top. Espalier-grown apple and fan-grown apricots are positioned against the fence. Climbing plants can also be trained, but this is mainly to ensure that they grow neatly, and they require much less pruning.

Apart from self-clinging climbers, such as ivy (*Hedera*) and Virginia creeper (*Parthenocissus*), others will need support and training along pergolas, trellis etc (*Clematis, Lonicera*). These will need to be anchored very firmly, as the mature plants can be quite heavy.

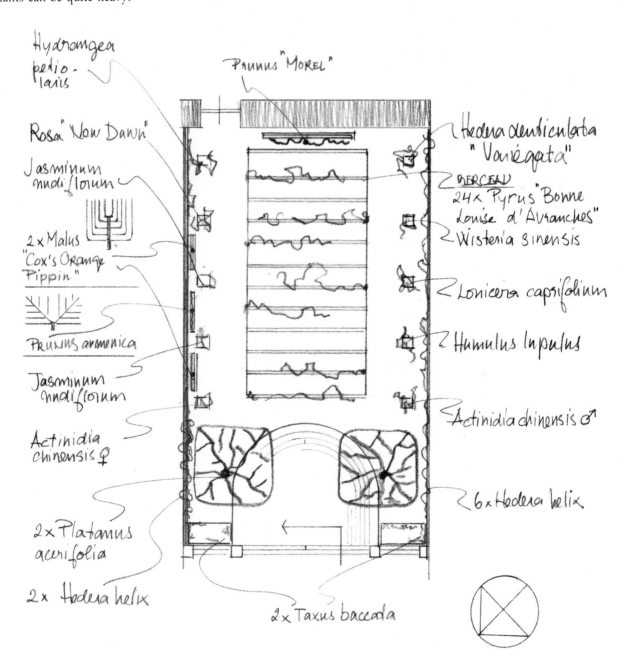

Hydrangea petiolaris

Rosa "New Dawn"

Jasminum nudiflorum

2 x Malus "Cox's Orange Pippin"

Prunus armenica

Jasminum nudiflorum

Actinidia chinensis ♀

2 x Platanus acrifolia

2 x Hedera helix

Prunus "Morel"

Hedera denticulata "Variegata"

BERCEAU
24 x Pyrus "Bonne Louise d'Avranches"

Wisteria sinensis

Lonicera caprifolium

Humulus lupulus

Actinidia chinensis ♂

6 x Hedera helix

2 x Taxus baccata

Actinidia arguta, Kiwi

Actinidia
Kiwi

⬚ ↕ 6-12 m ◯ ◐ ✿ 6-7 ⬡ 10-11

The fruit of *Actinidia*, indigenous in eastern Asia and the Himalayas, is generally known as the kiwi fruit. It was given this name in New Zealand because the shape and appearance are reminiscent of one of the indigenous birds, the kiwi, the national symbol of New Zealand. Three of the 40 different species produce edible fruits.
This is a dioecious climber, i.e., the male and female flowers appear on different plants. It is deciduous and has woody stems, beautifully shaped, attractive, round or heart-shaped, pointed, serrated leaves, white or brownish flowers and berry-like fruit which usually appear only after five years, (when they are abundant). The seeds only develop on female plants in large numbers, often radiating out. They are ready for picking in late autumn.
A. arguta, Kokuwa, is winter-hardy, up to 12 m tall, with white flowers up to 2 cm across, and sweet, edible, dark green, hairless fruits which turn brownish-red and are 2-3 cm across; "Bayern" has greenish-brown fruits.
A. chinensis, kiwi, Chinese gooseberry, is sensitive to frost and up to 9 m tall. The

young stems are hairy and brownish-red, it has leaves up to 20 cm long, sweet-smelling, creamy-white flowers, and edible, round or oblong, hairy, brown fruits, 5-7 cm long, with a delicate, fresh, sweet-sour taste.
A. kolomikta is winter-hardy and up to 6 m tall and has coloured leaves with a white and later pink tip, 12 cm long, small white flowers and delicious, sweet, bluish-black fruits. The plant branches out regularly, but grows slowly.
This plant is suitable for training against (warm) walls, in old trees, on pergolas, pillars, fences etc., in the sun or semi-shade, in moist, nutritious soil, rich in humus. For fruit formation, plant one male next to two female specimens. Remove dead and frozen branches. It does not need pruning. Propagate from cuttings in summer and seed.

Akebia

⊻ ↕ 6-10 m ◯ ⊘ ✿ 4-6 ✳

Akebia is indigenous in eastern Asia and comprises only two species. These attractive climbers can grow to a height of many metres with the help of vertical supports. This is a vigourous, woody-stemmed, semi-evergreen, twining plant with delicate groups of 3-5 leaves placed alternately, and fragrant clusters of flowers. In warmer climates it has fleshy, cucumber-like fruit, which is brownish-purple with a bluish tinge. *A. quinata*, 6-10 m tall, has thin, twining stems growing close together, and dense foliage consisting of purplish-brown leaves with five oval leaflets and slightly concealed, reddish-purple, fragrant clusters of flowers about 3 cm across, with a pinky-lilac calyx, deep purple petals, and purplish-brown fruit, 5-8 cm long. *A. trifoliata (A. lobata)* has slightly lobed leaves consisting of three leaflets, fragrant brown clusters of flowers and pale purple fruit.

This plant is very suitable for growing against walls, gates and pergolas, in the sun or semi-shade, in a sheltered position. It requires well-drained, nutritious soil. Cover young plants to protect against night frost. Carefully train plants along (vertical) supports (pergola, netting or wire). When the plant becomes bare at the bottom, a few stems can be pruned down to the main stem; do not prune back too hard, as it dislikes being pruned. Propagate by removing runners from roots, from cuttings (in summer), and from seed. Sensitive to root damage.

Akebia quinata

Actinidia kolomikta, Kiwi

11

Ampelopsis
Vine

⊠ ⫯ 6-10 m ○ ⊘ ⊛ 7-8 ⛀

Ampelopsis is indigenous in North America and eastern Asia. It comprises about 30 species, similar to Virginia creeper (*Parthenocissus*). A number of these can be cultivated in the garden with the necessary cover in winter.

This climbing shrub is deciduous, and grows like a vine with twining stems, red or yellow tendrils (Virginia creeper has sucker-like pads), and undivided, lobed, slightly serrated leaves. The attractive fruit develop only if it is very warm.

A. aconitifolia has delicate, bright, dark green, deeply lobed leaves, 10-13 cm across, and orange or yellow fruit.

A. brevipedunculata (syn. *A. heterophylla*) has lobed green leaves with white spots in varying shapes, and fruit which changes from a greenish to a bluish-purple colour; "Elegans" has reddish twigs and dark green, white and pink or red spotted leaves. It is also suitable as a house plant. It requires a light spot, protected from sunlight, and nutritious, well-drained soil. Keep moist at all times in summer, water regularly, feed every other week. In winter the leaves drop off. Place in a cool spot, water less and do not feed. Repot in spring and prune back.

A. japonica, Japanese Ivy, has green twigs and bright green lobed leaves. The plant clings to supports. It requires a slightly shady spot and nutritious soil. Protect in winter with a thick layer of peat, dry leaves and branches. Prune back in spring. Propagate from cuttings.

Ampelopsis brevipedunculata, Vine

Aristolochia
Birthwort

🌱 ↕ 5-10 m ○ ◐ ✾ 5-7 ❄ ⌷

Aristolochia is indigenous in (sub)tropical America, Africa and Asia, and temperate regions in North America. It comprises approximately 350 herbaceous and woody-stemmed species with attractive large leaves, and flowers like pipe bowls.
A. macrophylla (syn. *A. durior, A. sipho*) is a compact climber which is deciduous, with large, heart-shaped, overlapping leaves (up to 45 cm in diameter), and long-stemmed, greenish yellow or brownish, pipe-shaped flowers.
A. sempervirens (syn. *A. altissima*) is barely winter-hardy, though the roots are fairly winter-hardy. It is an evergreen, except in severe frost. The leaves are 5-10 cm long, and it has yellowish-brown flowers with darker stripes. Cover well in winter. It is cultivated as a screen, and is suitable for bowers, pergolas and north/west-facing walls. This plant requires a sunny or slightly shady spot, and moist soil containing clay. Water regularly and feed in spring. Support young plants and prune if necessary. Propagate by layering tendrils, and from seed. It is resistant to pollution.

Aristolochia sempervirens,
Birthwort

Aristolochia macrophylla,
Birthwort

Basella alba,
Ceylon spinach

Basella
Ceylon spinach

⬤ ↕ up to 6 m ◯ ✿ 5-6 🌡

The young leaves of *Basella*, which is indigenous in tropical Africa and Madagascar, can be used in the same way as spinach. Two of the six species are also cultivated as an ornamental plant. They are difficult to distinguish from each other and are sometimes classified as a single species. *B. rubra* is an annual twining climber with fleshy green or purple stems, and round or elliptical, alternating, shiny reddish leaves, thick flower stems ending in clusters of ear-shaped, red flowers and fleshy, deep red fruit; *B. rubra* var. *alba* has narrow, oval or lanceolate, dark green leaves and clusters of red flowers.

This is a fast-growing climber for pergolas and garden partitions (made of chicken wire etc.). It requires a sunny, not too windy spot in any fertile soil. Water in dry weather. It is also suitable as ground cover. Propagate from seed (early spring in heated greenhouse, 18-21° C for germination, then harden off at 15-20° C and plant outside in mid-May), and from cuttings.

Basella alba "Rubra",
Ceylon spinach

Bryonia cretica,
Bryony

Bryonia
Bryony

⬡ 🌿 ↕ 4 m ○ ◑ ⚙ 6-8 !

Bryonia cretica,
Bryony

Bryonia is found growing wild in hedges, copses, and dunes of central, western and southern Europe. Every part of the plant, especially the roots and berries, are extremely poisonous. If children inadvertently eat the berries, they should drink lots of milk and be taken to the doctor immediately. This fast-growing climber has a thick, tuberous rhizome growing underground. Long, thin stems develop from this every year, with unbranched creepers which curl up in a spiral when they attach themselves, so that the plant pulls itself up. It has heart-shaped, 3-5 lobed leaves and clusters of yellowish-green or white, green-veined flowers growing in the leaf axilla, and red or black berries, 7-8 mm in diameter.

B. alba, White bryony, is monoecious, has male and female flowers on the same plant, a yellow or white-green flowerhead and black berries.

B. cretica subsp. *dioica* (syn. *B. dioica*) is dioecious (male and female flowers do not grow on the same plant), and has a yellowish-white or yellowish-green flowerhead with five fused, spreading petals and red berries.

For bowers etc. in the sun or semi-shade, in sandy soil which is not too moist. Propagate from seed. Attracts bees.

15

Calystegia

◦ ↕ 1-5 m ◯ ❀ 6-9 ⚠

The flowers of *Calystegia*, which is indigenous in temperate regions of Europe, particularly Mediterranean regions, America and Asia, often open for only one day, or sometimes only for a few hours; the twining stems wind in a clockwise direction around other objects. In the past the roots and leaves were used for medicinal purposes. A number of species used to be classified under *Convolvulus*.

This rampant plant has spreading leaves and trumpet-shaped or double flowers in the leaf axilla, which usually grow on their own and are encased by two large bracts.

C. hederacea (syn. *C. pubescens, Convolvulus pubescens*), Chinese convolvulus, is a perennial with spreading roots, slightly hairy, sagittate leaves, broad bracts with folded edges, and double pinky-red flowers with a green calyx. Grow in a sheltered, warm spot against a fence.

C. sepium (syn. *Convolvulus sepium*), Bellbind, grows wild in hedgerows and copses, among reeds and along dykes. It is a perennial, spreading plant with branching roots which grow deep down, hairless leaves and delicate trumpet-shaped, white or sometimes pinky-red flowers on stems; the roots break easily and each piece of root continues to grow so that it is difficult to control the plant.

C. silvester (syn. *Convolvulus silvester*), Striped bindweed, has short, hairy leaves and trumpet-shaped, pinkish-red leaves.

C. soldanella (syn. *Convolvulus soldanella*), Sea bindweed, grows in the dunes. It has a creeping stem, thick kidney-shaped, blunt, shiny green leaves, and trumpet-shaped, pinkish-red flowers with white stripes, which open for only a few hours. It is resistant to salt water and blowing sand. This plant requires a dry, sunny, sheltered spot on a slope or against a fence. To prevent it from spreading out of control, place a deep circle of stones around it. Propagate from root cuttings and seed. Attracts bumblebees, bees, flies and moths.

Calystegia sepium,
Bellbind

Campsis
Trumpet creeper

🌿 ↕ 3-10 m ○ ◐ ❀ 5/7-9

Campsis is indigenous in the forests of eastern America and Asia. It comprises only two species and one hybrid. This tall climber winds round branches and trellises with aerial roots and twining shoots. The climbing shrub has woody stems with adventitious roots on the shade side, and delicate pinnate leaves with 7-9 leaflets. Yellow or red clusters of long, trumpet-shaped flowers grow at the ends of the new shoots.

C. grandiflora, Chinese trumpet vine, 3-6 m tall, is deciduous. The upper side of the leaf is hairy, and the bright red, drooping flowers in plumes are up to 7.5 cm long and have a crimson glow. This is a greenhouse plant, and can only be cultivated outside in warmer climates in a sunny, sheltered spot. Protect in winter.

C. radicans, trumpet honeysuckle, is a vigorous climber, and fairly winter-hardy (12-20 m tall), with orangey-red, sometimes yellow flowers, 6-8 cm long. Cultivars are less winter-hardy, e.g., "Atropurpurea", which has deep red flowers; "Flava", yellow; "Praecox", bright red.

C. x tagliabuana, a hybrid of the two species described above, occasionally winter-hardy, flowers profusely; "Madame Galen", large, pinkish-red flowers, orangey-red inside; "Rosea", pink; "Yellow Trumpet", yellow. Suitable for pergolas and (south-facing) walls, it requires a sunny, warm, sheltered spot, and well-drained, nutritious soil. Support young plants and protect the base against frost. In the first few years prune back frequently for a good shape, then in March/April, just above the height of the previous year. Propagate by layering and from cuttings.

Campsis grandiflora, Chinese trumpet

Campsis radicans "Flava",
Trumpet creeper

Celastrus
Bittersweet

🌿 ↕ 7-12 m ○ ◉ ❀ 8-11 ⚠ ✂

Celastrus is found in woods, bush vegetation and grassy slopes in Africa, Asia, America and Australia. Two of the approximately 30 species are cultivated as garden plants. When it grows around a tree, the plant can twine itself around quickly in such a way that it prevents the tree from developing. This climbing shrub is deciduous. It has woody stems, green leaves which turn a beautiful yellow in autumn, insignificant, pale green flowers, even after the leaves have fallen, and attractive, poisonous, dark yellow fruits, which eventually burst open, revealing orange or bright red seed covers.
C. orbiculatus (syn. *C. articulatus*), Oriental bittersweet, monoecious and dioecious, grows up to 12 m tall in various shapes and has pointed, serrated leaves, greenish clusters of flowers in the axilla, and yellow fruits with a bright red seed cover.
C. scandens, American bittersweet, is dioecious, 6-10 m tall, with greenish plumes at the end of the stems and yellowish-orange fruits with an orangey-red seed cover.
This plant grows quickly and is suitable for pergolas, pillars, fences and walls.
To encourage fruit formation, plant female and male specimens in sun or semi-shade in any soil rich in humus. Support, prune back if necessary, and remove dead wood in winter. Stems with ripe berries can be kept for several weeks in water; cut before the fruit bursts open. Propagate by layering, from cuttings (summer or winter) and from seed.

Celastrus orbiculatus,
Bittersweet

Chaenomeles
Flowering quince, Japonica

🌿 ↕ 1-2,5 m ○ ◐ ✿ 3-5/6 ❀ ❋

Chaenomeles is indigenous in eastern Asia, and comprises three species, which differ greatly in the shape and colour of their flowers and the way in which they grow, as well as many varieties. They are beautiful garden shrubs. Low varieties can be used as ground cover, while slightly taller ones can be grown in front of larger shrubs as a specimen plant or as a hedge. A number of attractive varieties can be trained along walls if they are carefully tied back and pruned.

This branching shrub is deciduous. It is often thorny and has alternating or closely packed, short-stemmed, serrated, shiny dark-green leaves, numerous short-stemmed, single or (semi-double) white, pink or red flowers, which grow on their own or in clusters, with five petals and sepals, and yellow, apple or pear-shaped fruit (suitable for making jam).

C. cathayensis, up to 3 m tall, with lanceolate leaves, 8-12 cm long, with downy hair on the underside, white flowers and large fruit.

C. speciosa, up to 2 m tall, flowers from March to May. It has long, formidable thorns, hairless, shiny, dark green, oval or oblong greatly serrated leaves, dish-shaped, white, pink, or red flowers, 1-4 cm across, and aromatic yellow or greenish-yellow fruit, 8 cm long; "Moerloosei" has pale pink clusters of flowers; "Nivalis" has bright white flowers; "Umbilicata" has dark, pinky-red flowers.

C. x superba hybrids flower profusely and include "Boule de Feu", up to 2.5 m tall, with crimson flowers (May) and fragrant fruit; "Clementine", up to 1.5 m tall, orangey-red flowers; "Crimson and Gold", up to 1 m tall, dark red; "Elly Mosel", up to 1 m tall, bright red (March); "Fire Dance", up to 1.25 m tall, a broad shrub with very large, dark red flowers; "Pink Lady", pink flowers; "Rowallane", up to 1.3 m tall, a broad shrub, bright red.

It requires a sunny spot or semi-shade, protect early flowerers, grow in any fertile soil, train the plant along the wall, e.g., by tying it back, prune back every year after flowering, remove ground shoots (take care: the plant flowers on stems more than one year old). Propagate from seed (spring and autumn).

Chaenomeles x superba, Flowering quince

Chaenomeles, Flowering quince

Clematis, "Nelly Moser"

Clematis
Old man's beard, Traveller's joy

🌱 ↕ 2-10 m ○ ◑ ✺ 4/5-9/10 !

Clematis is found throughout the world and comprises about 400 species, as well as many cultivars, including a large number of climbing or creeping (semi-)shrubs;
C. vitalba, Old man's beard, can be found growing wild in the Netherlands (Limburg, eastern river area), twining around hedges and the undergrowth.
This is a vigorous climber with twining stems. It is deciduous, comes in various shapes, and flowers profusely with flat or bell-shaped flowers, in all sorts of shades of pink, red, blue, purple and white.
Small-flowered varieties can also be yellow. After flowering, there are often downy seed heads, which remain on the plant long into the winter.
C. alpina is indigenous in mountain regions in central and southern Europe. It is winter-hardy and does not grow very fast. It is up to 2.5 m tall (after many years, 3.5 m tall). It flowers in May/June to August, and

Clematis,
"Duchess of Edinburgh"

has three-lobed, serrated leaves, attractive, small, pendent, dish-shaped, violet flowers in the leaf axilla, and fluffy seed heads; *C. alpina* subsp. *sibirica* has pale yellow flowers and narrower petals; "Ruby" has dark, pinky-red flowers; "White Moth" has semi-double white flowers; suitable for low fences, walls etc, in shade or semi-shade in well-drained soil. Pruning is not really necessary, but if it is pruned, this should be done after flowering (not in autumn or winter, because of bud formation), and the fluffy seed heads will not appear.
C. armandii, China, evergreen, is not or is only slightly winter-hardy, and is 5-6 (to 10) m tall. It flowers in April/May, has shiny, dark green, oblong leaves consisting of three leaflets, and fragrant white or pink clusters of flowers 3-6 cm across;
C. armandii "Apple Blossom" has leaves which turn a bronze colour and pinkish-white flowers; "Snowdrift" has bright white flowers; it requires a warm, sheltered spot in the sun or semi-shade in any type of soil. Prune in spring and cover in winter.
C. cirrhosa, Mediterranean regions, evergreen, not winter-hardy, grows up to 4 m tall. It flowers in February/April to May, and has leathery, single or lobed, oval, serrated leaves, cream or whitish-yellow, pendent, dish-shaped flowers with red dots inside, 3-5 cm across, and silky seed heads; *C. cirrhosa* var. *balearica* has more delicately divided leaves which turn more purple in winter, and fragrant flowers; it requires a warm, sunny, sheltered spot in any slightly dry soil. Prune in early spring, cover in winter.
• *C. x durandii* is a cross of *C. integrifolia* and *C.* "Jackmanii". It is a winter-hardy, spreading plant, up to 2.5 m tall, and flowers from June to September. It has a woody base, short-stemmed, single, smooth-edged leaves, deep violet flowers, 8-12 cm across, which grow singly and have a bunch of yellow stamens in the heart. Bind or support with other plants, grow in sun or semi-shade in any soil. Prune in spring and late summer.
C. flammula, Mediterranean region, is moderately or very winter-hardy, and 4-5 m tall. It flowers from July to October, has a woody base, multipinnate, elliptical leaves, usually smooth-edged, and fragrant white flowerheads. It requires a warm, sheltered spot in sun or semi-shade in any soil. Prune back in spring, cover in winter.
C. florida hybrids, semi winter-hardy, 1-2.5 m tall, flower from May to June with double flowers up to 8 cm across. "Alba Plena" has double, whitish-green flowers; "Duchess of Edinburgh", white fragrant flowers; "Sieboldi", white flowers with a tuft of purple stamens in the heart; it

Clematis, "J.L. Delbart",

Clematis, "Gipsy Queen"

satin-pink flowers; "Gipsy Queen", up to
5 m tall, reddish-purple flowers with red
veins; "Hagley hybrid", dark pink flowers
turning light pink; "Jackmanii Alba", white
double, later single flowers; "Jackmannii
Superba", dark purplish-blue, semi-double,
later single flowers; "Lady Betty Balfour",
flowers August to October, violet; "Madame
Baron Veillard", July to August,
purplish-pink; "Niobe", dark red; "Perle
d'Azure", is a vigorous plant up to 4.5 m
tall, with pale blue flowers up to 15 cm
across; they require a sheltered spot in the
sun or semi-shade, and any type of soil.
Prune back hard in spring, and cover lightly
at the beginning of winter.
C. lanuginosa hybrids, 2-4 m tall, flower
from June to September/October, with
brightly coloured flowers with 6-8 petals:
"Blue Gem" has azure flowers; "Crimson
King", red flowers with brown stamens;
"Henryi", pure white; "Lawsoniana", bright
lilac flowers up to 20 cm across; "Madame
le Coultre", flowers profusely from May to
September, with white flowers; "Nelly Moser",
has pinkish-white flowers, 18 cm across
with red veins and red stamens, grow in
light shade; "Sensation", satin red; "The
President", large bronze leaves, dark purplish-
blue flowers; "W.E. Gladstone", lilac blue;
"William Kennet", dark lavender blue; they
require a sunny or slightly shady spot, prune
in early spring and cover lightly in winter.
C. macropetela is indigenous in Siberia and
northern China. This plant is deciduous,
winter-hardy, and grows up to 3 m tall. It
flowers from May to August. The leaves are
double tripinnate and serrated, and the
pendent, bell-shaped, lilac-blue flowers are
up to 5 cm across and have four petals and
a large number of narrow honey glands; "Blue
Bird", violet-blue flowers; "Maidwell Hall",
dark violet; "Rödklokke", pinkish-red; they
require a sunny or slightly shady spot in any
soil. Prune back if necessary after flowering.
C. montana, from the Himalayas. This
strong, powerful climber is winter-hardy,
deciduous, and flowers profusely from April
to June. It grows 6-10 m tall, and has
tripinnate, oval, serrated leaves on stems,
and white or pink flowers, 4 cm across,
with four spreading petals which grow in
groups of three or four; *C. montana* var.
Rubens has dark green leaves and larger pink
or pinkish-white flowers; "Alexander" has
white flowers; "Elizabeth" has slightly
fragrant, whitish-pink flowers; "Mayleen",
light pink; "Tetrarose", bronze leaves and
large pinkish-red flowers up to 8 cm across;
they are suitable for pergolas, sheds and
north-facing walls in semi-shade, and will
grow in any slightly dry soil. Prune back if
necessary immediately after flowering.
C. patens hybrids, up to 4 m tall, flower
from May to June and August to September;

Clematis,
"Ernest Markham"

Clematis, "Niobe"

requires a sunny, sheltered spot. Remove
old flowering stems, prune back hard after
flowering (August/September), cover lightly
in winter.
C. x jackmanii (syn. *C.* "Jackmanii") is a
cross of *C. lanuginosa* and *C. viticella*). It is
deciduous, grows up to 3.5 m tall, and
flowers from July to September. The leaves
consist of three leaflets, the dark,
purplish-blue flowers are 10-13 cm across:
hybrids include "Comtesse de Bouchard",
grows rapidly, flowers profusely with

"Barbara Jackmann" has large violet flowers with purple stripes, up to 15 cm across, and does not grow in full sunlight; "Bees Jubilee" is dark purplish-pink with lighter coloured veins; "Dr. Ruppel" is light pink with dark pink veins; "Laserstern", May to June, has large dark blue flowers; "Vyvyan Pennell", double, dark, purplish-blue flowers up to 20 cm across, and slightly lighter blooms when it flowers for the second time. Not too much shade; they require a sunny or shady spot in any soil. Prune occasionally after flowering and cover lightly in winter.

C. tangutica from Central Asia, is a winter-hardy, vigorous climber, which grows up to 3 m tall. It flowers from June/August to October, and has pinnate, coarsely serrated, elliptical, bright green leaves, single, nodding, bell-shaped golden-yellow flowers, and beautiful silvery-green fluffy seed heads turning greyish-brown, which last all winter; "Aureolin" has larger yellow flowers; they are suitable for gates, trellises, walls, in sunny or slightly shady spots, in any soil. Prune at the end of the winter to keep fluffy seed heads.

C. vitalba, Europe, is a winter-hardy, vigorous, rapidly growing, spreading plant, 10-12 m tall. It flowers from June to August, has pairs of pinnate leaves consisting of oval, coarsely serrated or smooth-edged, sometimes lobed leaflets, and large, creamy flowerheads consisting of numerous small, fragrant flowers which grow in the leaf axilla or at the end of the stem. The beautiful silvery fluffy seed heads turn grey, and last until spring; they are suitable for larger gardens, pergolas, sheds etc. Do not plant next to weaker species. They require semi-shade and the soil should not be too dry. Prune in spring, but the plant can rapidly self-seed.

C. viticella, southeast Europe, is a winter-hardy plant which grows 3-4 m tall and flowers from June to September. It has hairy, reddish-brown stems, leaves with deeply indented oval leaflets, and nodding, purplish-red flowers, 4-7 cm across, which grow on stems and have four spreading petals; "Alba Luxurians" green or white flowers; "Kermesina" grows up to 2 m tall and has burgundy flowers; "Madame Jules Correvon" numerous dark red flowers, prune back hard; "Margot Koster" dark pink flowers with pale pink stripes, prune back hard; "Minuet" grows up to 8 m tall, and has pinkish-red flowers with broad white stripes, prune back hard; they are suitable for walls, pergolas, in (rose) bushes and trees, in full sunlight, in well-drained soil. Prune in spring. Depending on the height, these plants are suitable for low or high fences, slopes, walls, pergolas, sheds, in trees and shrubs which are bare at the bottom etc. They require a sunny or semi-shady spot and nutritious, rich in lime and soil

humus. The attachments should be the wall (4 cm from). Plant in a large hole, feed in the autumn. Late flowering varieties can be pruned back to approximately 100 cm above ground level. Propagate from cuttings (June to July), using rooting powder, by layering woody stems (May to June) and from seed.

Clematis, "Bees Jubilee"

Clematis, "Margot Koster"

Clianthus

⬚ ↕ 1,8-3 m ○ ❀ 5-8

Clianthus is indigenous in New Zealand and Australia. It comprises only two species which flower in a striking way. In temperate regions they have to be overwintered in frost-free conditions, and they are sometimes cultivated as annuals. This shrub-like plant has horizontal or vertical stems, herbaceous, hairy shoots, and compound, greyish-green leaves covered with fine hair on the underside, consisting of 9-21 whorls of oblong, oval leaflets. It has papilonaceous flowerheads, consisting of one standing petal (flag), two petals which grow outwards (swords) and two fused into a boat shape (heel). They grow in clusters of four to five bright red flowers with a black heart, or plain red, pink, or white flowers; it has pod-like fruits up to 6 cm long.

C. puniceus can grow up to 3 m tall with support. It has climbing stems and bright red, pink, or creamy flowers up to 8 cm long; "Albus" has bright white flowers. Plant in a pot against a south-facing wall in full sunlight, in well-drained, alkaline, sandy, stony soil, and train against the wall. It is not resistant to moisture and cold. Water sparingly (root rot). Dig up in October and overwinter in a light, cool, frost-free place. Propagate from seed (spring, in a heated greenhouse).

Clianthus puniceus "Roseus"

24

Cobaea

· ↕ 3-6 m ○ ◎ 6/7-9 ⊡

Cobaea is indigenous in tropical regions of America. It comprises about 18 perennial climbing species, of which *C. scandens* is often cultivated in Europe as an annual garden plant.
C. scandens, Cup-and-sauver vine, a woody-stemmed climber, grows up to 12 m tall in Mexico. Cultivated varieties grow up to 6 m tall. It is a fast-growing, herbaceous annual plant which is not winter-hardy, with flexible, twining stems, compound, oval leaves on stems, spiralling tendrils from the leaf axilla, and bell-shaped flowers, 5-6 cm across, which are green at first, and later turn deep purple, and which grow singly in the leaf axilla; "Alba" has white flowers; "Variegata", purple flowers, variegated leaves.
Suitable for pergolas (south-facing), walls, trellises etc. This plant requires a sunny spot in well-drained, moist soil, rich in humus. Water liberally in warm weather.

Cobaea scandens

If necessary, overwinter in a large pot after flowering (September/October) in a frost-free place. Water sparingly and plant out again in mid-May. Propagate from seed under glass, germinate at 15-20° C, keep seedlings at 12-15° C, support and plant out in mid-May.

Cobaea scandens "Alba"

25

Codonopsis tangshen

the attractive pendent flowers, which are best seen from below, compensate for this. It is a spreading plant with thick, fleshy roots, whorls of short-stemmed, oval, pale green leaves, and pendent, bell-shaped, white, yellow or blue flowers marked inside with beautiful veining.

C. rotundifolia, up to 1 m tall, has twining, branching stems, spreading, oval, pointed, serrated leaves which are hairy on the underside, and pale, yellowish-green flowers with brown veins.

C. tangshen, up to 1 m tall, has climbing, twining stems, broad, lanceolate, pointed, coarsely serrated leaves, and greenish flowers up to 5 cm across with purplish veins and a purple heart.

C. vinciflora is very similar to the above species, but has smaller flowers. It is suitable for rockeries. Plant it higher up so that the flowers come into their own best between and trained along large rocks.

Do not plant too close to other shrubs, as it can take over. It requires a sunny spot and loamy soil, rich in humus. Do not move (damage to roots). Propagate from seed (spring).

Codonopsis

○ ↕ 50-180 ○ ◑ ✿ 6-7

Codonopsis is indigenous in central and eastern Asia. It comprises about 20 species, of which some are climbing or creeping plants. It has a rather unpleasant smell, but

Codonopsis convulacea

Cucurbita
Ornamental gourd

· ↕ 2-6 m ○ ✤ 6-9 ▭

Cucurbita, indigenous in North and South America, comprises about 27 species, of which a number produce well-known vegetables, such as pumpkins and courgettes. It is also used as ornamental ground cover and can look very attractive trained along trellises, fences and walls. This is an annual or perennial herbaceous climber, with large, palmate, veined leaves, big, single, yellow flowers which usually flower for only one day, and large, often strikingly formed fruit.

C. maxima "Turbaniformis" is a powerful annual climber with round stems, twining shoots, almost round, slightly serrated leaves, large yellow flowers with spreading, pointed petals slightly folded back, and inedible orange fruit with an orange coloured growth on the top.

C. pepo, the ornamental gourd, is a bushy annual with angular, spiny stems, long tendrils, broad, triangular, deeply lobed, spiny leaves, yellow trumpet-shaped flowers and inedible fruit in various shapes (which resemble apples, pears, oranges, cones or bottles) with leathery, multicoloured, warty

or wrinkled skins. They are dried for decorative purposes.

Grow against a fence or chicken wire structure in a sunny spot in nutritious, well-drained soil. Water liberally and feed occasionally. Sow in early April (in a warm place, 20° C), plant out mid-May.

Cucurbita maxima,
Ornamental gourd

Cucurbita maxima
"Turbaniformis",
Ornamental gourd

27

Cydonia oblonga,
Quince

Cydonia
Quince

🌱 ↕ 1,5-3 m ○ ◐ ✿ 5-6 ❀ 6-10

Cydonia originates in western Asia and comprises only one species, *C. oblonga*, which has been cultivated in Europe for a long time, both for its fruit and as an ornamental tree. It can be trained on a special structure and pruned to create a beautiful, fragrant, fruiting hedge.
C. oblonga (syn. *Pyrus oblonga*) is a thornless shrub up to 3 m tall, with short-stemmed, oval, smooth-edged leaves, 5-11 cm long, which are dark green on the upper side and white or grey felted underneath. It has single, white or pink flowers up to 4 cm across on young shoots in the leaf axilla, and after two or three years, it produces fragrant apple or pear-shaped, soft-haired, golden-yellow fruits 8 cm long, which can be harvested from October and are suitable for making jams, jellies, etc. *C. oblonga* "Vranje" has large, fragrant, pale yellow fruits.

Decumaria

Plant young trees at the end of March in a
sheltered, sunny, or semi-shady spot, in soil
rich in humus and not too dry, at intervals
of 2-2.5 m, with a structure for training the
trees. Place supports (up to 60/70 cm in the
ground; the outer posts at an angle for extra
strength), and stretch wires across
(approximately 50 cm from the ground, and
up to approximately 2 m). Train one shoot
to the left and one to the right, and trim the
middle shoot. In subsequent years, bind the
two strongest side shoots to the right and
left in July/August. Trim the middle shoot
again, remove all the other shoots. When
the middle shoot has reached the top wire,
tie it down and bend over, remove shoots
which are growing to the front or back and
thin out (not the young shoots bearing
fruit). Propagate from seed and cuttings.

Decumaria

 up to 10 m ○ ◐ ◉ ✾ 5-6

Decumaria is indigenous in the United
States and Central China. It comprises only
two species, one of which is reasonably
winter-hardy.
It is a deciduous or evergreen,
woody-stemmed climber with thin stems
and adventitious roots, whorls of slightly
serrated leaves with stems, and compact
clusters of fragrant white fertile flowers
which grow at the end of the stems.
D. barbara is semi-deciduous, resistant to
mild winters, and up to 10 m tall. It has
shiny green, oval, pointed leaves, 5-10 cm
long, slightly hairy underneath, and round
white clusters of flowers, 5-10 cm across. It
is also suitable as ground cover.
This is an attractive, rather slow-growing
climber for walls, fences and on trees and
other supports, in the sun or shade, in
moist, nutritious soil. Prune only if
necessary to retain shape, and cover in
winter. Propagate from seed (unheated
greenhouse) and cuttings in summer.

Eccremocarpus

○  2-3(-5) m ○ ✾ 6-10

*Eccremocarpus scaber
"Tresco hybridis"*

Eccremocarpus, indigenous in Chile and
Peru, comprises five perennial species, one
of which is cultivated in Europe as a garden
plant, often as an annual in temperate regions.
This evergreen climber is not winter-hardy.
It has slightly woody stems, whorls of
compound, lobed or pinnate leaves, and
clusters of asymmetrical, tubular, yellow,
orange or red flowers.
E. scaber, Glory vine, grows rapidly and
flowers profusely. It has leafy stems,
branching tendrils, bipinnate leaves
consisting of oval, irregularly lobed leaflets,
and pendent racemes of tubular, bright
orange flowers which bell out at the base;
"Aureus" has golden-yellow flowers;
"Carmineus", crimson; "Ruber", dark red;
"Tresco", combination, mixed seeds of
yellow, pink and purple varieties.
This plant is suitable for (south-facing)
walls, gates, pergolas etc. Grow in a sunny
sheltered spot, in well-drained, nutritious,
moist soil. The plant can be kept through
the winter, if it is not too cold. In that case,
prune back completely and cover thoroughly.
It is also possible to lift the tuber (in
autumn) and store it in a frost-free place for
the winter. Plant out in mid-May. Propagate
from seed in a heated greenhouse (February/
March) and plant out at the end of May.

Euonymus

🌿 ↕ 0,5-3 m ○ ◉ ✿ 6-7

There are over 170 species of *Euonymus*,
including evergeen and deciduous shrubs,
a number which are used as ground cover,
and climbing plants, such as *E. fortunei*,
from China, Japan and Korea, and its
cultivars. It has red fruit in the shape and
colour of Roman Catholic cardinals' hats.
This fruit is popular with thrushes, starlings
and robins. In the European climate this
species does not often flower and bear fruit.
E. fortunei is an evergreen, woody-stemmed,
climbing or creeping shrub with adventitious
roots, which is occasionally winter-hardy.
It grows up to 3 m tall against a wall, with
spreading horizontal stems. It has dull,
green serrated leaves with lighter veins and
an orange glow in winter. *E. fortunei* var.
radicans (syn. *E. radicans*) has dark green
leaves; "Carrierei" grows up to 2.5 m tall
and has shiny green leaves; "Coloratus" has
bright green leaves which turn deep purple,
and greenish-yellow umbels of small
flowers; "Emerald Gaiety" is up to 1.5 m
tall, and has green leaves with silvery white
margins; "Emerald 'n Gold" is up to 50 cm
tall, with green leaves with a broad
yellowish-white margin; "Kewensis", a
dwarf variety, has thin stems, small green
leaves, and is suitable for rockeries and low
walls; "Variegatus" (syn. "Gracilis", "Silver
Gem") is up to 50 cm tall, with green leaves
spotted with cream and a pink glow;
"Vegetus" has shiny dark green leaves and
many fruits.
This plant is suitable for (low) walls.
Grow in the sun or semi-shade in moist,
nutritious soil. Occasionally prune back
older specimens. Propagate from cuttings
(spring and August) and by dividing roots.

top: Euonymus fortunei "Emerald 'n Gold"

Euonymus fortunei "Vegetus"

Fallopia aubertii,
Knotweed

Fallopia
Knotweed

○ | 10-15 m ↔ up to 3 m ○ ◐ ✿ 7-10

Fallopia is indigenous in the former Soviet Union, amongst other places. There is some confusion regarding the species which should be classified in this genus; they are sometimes classified under *Polygonum* or *Bilderdykia*, and the common names are also confused.
This is a deciduous, woody-stemmed climber, and grows quickly with long shoots. It has spreading, triangular leaves and airy, greenish-white panicles of flowers. It can cover entire walls, sheds and fences, including the gutters, windows, doors etc.
Fallopia aubertii (syn. *Polygonum aubertii, Bilderdykia aubertii*), Baby's breath, has reddish stems more than 10 m long, which wind around everything, triangular, pointed leaves with a heart-shaped base, and pendent, coarse-haired panicles of greenish-white flowers which often turn pink later.

Fallopia baldschuanica (syn. *Polygonum baldschuanicum, Bilderdykia baldschuanica*), Mile-a-minute plant, has branches up to 15 m long, large, long panicles of fragrant, greenish-white flowers with a reddish glow, which are more erect. Attracts bees.
This is an easy plant to grow, which spreads rapidly, e.g., for camouflaging tree trunks or walls which have become ugly. Grow in the sun (for more profuse flowering) or shade, in any nutritious soil. Prune back hard in spring. Propagate from cuttings (July/August) and from seed.

Ficus
Fig

⛏ ⬆ up to 4 m ○ ✿ 7-8

Ficus, indigenous in tropical and subtropical regions, is a very large genus, comprising a large diversity of shrubs, trees, creeping and climbing plants. All the species have stems and leaves which contain a milky juice. Some species produce edible fruits, including the well-known figs.

F. carica, with its beautiful leaves and delicious fruit is a common tree in streets and parks in hot countries; it is moderately winter-hardy, and trained against a south-facing wall it will tolerate some frost in colder regions. However, the harvest depends largely on the weather; if there is little sun, a long dry period, or great fluctuations in temperature, the fruit will not ripen very well, and will drop off. The fig is a false fruit; the inflorescence consists of a hollow, pear-shaped receptacle (the edges grow towards each other and a small opening, sealed with scales, connects it with the outside world), and inside there are hundreds of small flowers on the sides which later change into the true fruit, the pips of the fig. There are male and female fig trees, and it is the latter which produce fruit after being fertilized by the fig gall wasp. Nowadays there are also varieties with unfertilized figs, i.e., without pips.

F. carica, the common fig, is an evergreen, deciduous tree, in warm areas, with attractive, palmate, irregularly deeply indented leaves with three to four blunt lobes and round, oval or pear-shaped, delicious yellowish-green or golden yellow fruits which turn brownish-red or purplish-blue and are 5-8 cm across, growing in the leaf axilla. They can be harvested several times a year. The larger summer figs develop in the previous autumn and have a long time to mature.

This tree is suitable for training against a warm, south or west-facing wall, in sandy soil mixed with clay or loam, and well-rotted cow manure. After the second year, prune back to the ground (wear gloves for protection against the milky juice). Train up the strong shoots which appear after this. If necessary, protect against frost. Propagate from winter cuttings and by layering.

Ficus carica, Fig

Hedera
Ivy

☁ ! 6-20 m ◐ ● ❀ 9-10 ❋ 9-2 !

Hedera is indigenous in Europe, North
Africa and Asia. It is one of the best known
climbers for walls, rockeries and tree trunks.
It also serves as attractive green, leafy
ground cover beneath dark trees.
This woody, self-clinging, evergreen climber
matures very slowly. It has infertile, scaly,
hairy stems with countless adventitious
roots with which the plant anchors onto
trees or walls, and long-stemmed,
heart-shaped, slightly lobed leaves which
turn to the sun, and are thin and light green
at first, and later turn darker and leathery.
Fertile stems (only in mature specimens) at
the tips, no adventitious roots, with oval,
unlobed leaves in every direction, and
semi-circular, greenish-yellow umbels of
flowers on stems, which are very popular
with flies, bees and butterflies. They have
green, and later black berries which are
popular with birds.
H. *algeriensis*, "Gloire de Marengo" (syn.
H. canariensis "Variegata") is only slightly
winter-hardy. It has red stems and leaf stalks,
large three to five-lobed, oval, green leaves,
up to 20 cm long, with a white margin and
a heart-shaped base; it is also suitable as a
house plant in a spot that is not too warm.
H. *colchica*, Persian ivy, is winter-hardy,
with scaly, slightly lobed or unlobed, sometimes serrated, bright green leaves; "Dentata"
is winter-hardy, with light green serrated
leaves; "Dentata variegata" is slightly
winter-hardy, with coloured greenish-white
or cream leaves, suitable against a heated
wall; "Sulphur Heart" is winter-hardy with
coloured yellowish-green leaves.
H. *helix*, Common ivy, is winter-hardy,
with creeping or climbing, star-shaped,
hairy stems, and three to five-lobed, dark
green leaves, unlobed on the flowering
branches, where they have smooth margins
and black fruit. Some cultivars are
winter-hardy, and include "Buttercup",
yellow or yellowish-green leaves; "Eva",
green leaves, spotted with white; "Glacier",
greyish-green leaves with a pink margin;
"Gold-heart", green leaves with a yellow
heart; "Marmorata", green leaves with
yellow spots; "Pedata", deeply indented,
five- lobed leaves; "Sagittifolia", attractive
green, narrow-lobed, sagittate leaves;
H. *helix* subsp. *poetarum*, paler green, less
indented leaves, orange fruit.
H. *hibernica* (syn. *H. helix* "Hibernica"),
Irish ivy, is winter-hardy, with star-shaped,
hairy stems, and larger, heart-shaped, lobed,
light green veined leaves.

This is a strong climber for walls, sheds, etc.
Plant in light shade or shade in any
nutritious soil. Feed in spring, prune back
hard every other year (spring). Propagate
from cuttings.

*Hedera colchica
"Dentata Variegata",
Ivy*

Hedera helix "Goldheart", Ivy

Humulus japonicus,
Hop

Humulus

Hop

• ○ ↕ 1-6 m ○ ⊘ ✿ 7-8

Humulus is found throughout the northern hemisphere and is cultivated in several countries for lupuline, the substance secreted by the glands on the bracts of the hops, which give beer its characteristic (hop-like) taste.

This dioecious twining plant has long, rough stems which wind in a clockwise direction, and whorls of attractive, palmate serrated leaves. The male plant has long, branching, greenish clusters of flowers in the leaf axilla; the female plant has flower spikes in the axilla of the bracts.

After flowering, these develop into oval, greenish-yellow hops.

H. japonicus (syn. *H. scandens*) is an annual plant up to 4 m tall, with large, deeply indented, five to seven-lobed leaves, up to 20 cm long; "Variegata" has white, coloured leaves. It is a vigorous, fast-growing plant for pergolas, gates, roofs, sheds etc., and will grow in any soil, even soil poor in nutrients, in the sun or light shade.

It dies off completely every year. Propagate from seed.

H. lupulus, common hop, is a perennial spreading plant up to 6 m tall, with a creeping rhizome, and three to five-lobed leaves. The stems die off in winter and new shoots form in spring. Suitable for a woodland environment, it winds round tree trunks and can be grown against walls with support in a sunny or slightly shady spot in moist, nutritious soil. Propagate by dividing rhizomes and from seed.

Humulus lupulus
"Aureus", Hop

Hydrangea

⊾ ⬍ 5-20 m ◑ ◉ ✾ 6-7 ✳

Hydrangea is indigenous in Asia, North and Central America, amongst other places. It comprises about 80 species, mainly beautifully flowering woody shrubs and trees, and a few climbers. It is resistant to air pollution.

H. anomela subsp. *Petiolaris* (syn. *H. petiolaris*, *H. scandens*), climbing hydrangea, is a self-clinging, winter-hardy plant. It grows slowly for the first two years, then more quickly, and flowers profusely. It has light brown, attractively scaly stems, with bunches of adventitious roots and whorls of oval, serrated leaves, 15 cm long, on stems. The umbels of white, small, fertile and slightly larger infertile flowers, are 20-25 cm across.

This plant is very suitable for covering north-facing walls, and also looks good in old trees; plant in a shady spot in moist soil rich in humus. Only prune for a flat shape. Remove branches which grow slowly, or dead or trapped branches. In the first year, cover lightly in winter, and feed in the growing season (spring). Propagate from top cuttings in spring.

Hydrangea petiolaris

35

Ipomoea tricolor
"Heavenly blue"

related genera such as *Pharbitis* and *Quamoclit*; the prolifically flowering plants are often planted as annuals, and the beautiful flowers often open for only one day.
This annual or perennial climbing or creeping plant has spreading (un)divided, sometimes lobed leaves and beautiful bell-shaped or tubular flowers.
I. purpurea, common morning glory, is an annual which grows up to 4 m tall, with long-stemmed, slightly hairy, heart-shaped or oval, smooth-edged leaves, and groups of three to five trumpet-shaped, purplish-red, pink, blue or white flowers, up to 8 cm across, growing in the leaf axilla.
I. tricolor (syn. *I. rubrocoerulea*) is a perennial plant cultivated as an annual, up to 3 m tall, with thick greyish-green, round or oval leaves, and funnel-shaped, bluish-purple flowers, 8-10 cm long, with a white corolla; "Heavenly Blue" flowers early with azure or purplish-red flowers. This is a fast-growing plant suitable for growing against gates, pergolas, chicken wire, the railings of balconies, or south-facing walls (with a supporting structure) in a sheltered, sunny spot in nutritious soil, rich in humus. Propagate from seed sown under glass (March/April). Tie back young plants.

Ipomoea

• ⌈↓⌉ 2-4 m ○ ✻ 7-10

Ipomoea is mainly indigenous in tropical regions in Central and South America. It is sometimes confused with closely

Ipomoea acuminata

Jasminum
Jasmine

⚘ ↕ 2,5-6 m ○ ◐ ✿ 12-3/7-9

Jasminum is indigenous in tropical and subtropical regions in Asia. It comprises about 300 species of woody-stemmed plants, including many climbing and trailing plants. Only a few species, such as *J. nudiflorum*, are really winter-hardy; a few others can survive night frost if properly covered. This climbing or trailing shrub has winding shoots, or long, thin, limp stems, usually compound leaves in whorls or spreading, and often fragrant white or yellow flowers with a long, narrow corolla and spreading petals.

J. nudiflorum, Winter jasmine, is a deciduous, winter-hardy plant. It grows up to 2.5 m tall, and has thin, green, angular stems. The dark green leaves consist of three leaflets and appear in April. From December (in mild winters), slightly fragrant, golden yellow flowers appear on the wood over a year old along the entire length of the bare stems; stems with buds will flower indoors and keep for a long time in water. Remove shoots when they have finished flowering.

J. officinale, common jasmine, is not really winter-hardy. It is deciduous, grows up to 3 m tall, and has pinnate, compound leaves. It flowers from July to September with fragrant white flowers. This plant thrives best against a heated wall, in a sunny sheltered spot which is not too moist. Cover the base well in winter. It is also suitable for an unheated greenhouse or as a house plant.

J. x stephanense is not really winter-hardy. It grows to 3 m tall and flowers from June to July. It has twining stems, large, yellowish-green leaves consisting of three to five leaflets and pale pink flowers in clusters. Good winter covering is essential. This plant is suitable for walls, tied to trellises or supporting wire, arches and banks. It requires a sunny or slightly shady, warm, sheltered spot, and soil rich in humus which is not too dry. Plant in large holes. Propagate from top cuttings (May/July), by layering and from seed.

Jasminum nudiflorum,
Winter jasmine

Lathyrus odoratus
"Patio mix"

left:
Lathyrus odoratus
"Butterfly"
right:
Lathyrus odoratus
"Deep red"

Lathyrus

○ • ↕ 0,5-3 m ○ ◐ ✿ 6-10 ✂

Lathyrus is indigenous in temperate, warm regions of the northern hemisphere and South America. It comprises about 130 species; *L. pratensis*, L. silvestris, Everlasting pea, and *L. vernus* grow wild in the Netherlands. Species which are cultivated in the garden in particular include the hardy perennial, *L. latifolius*, and the wonderfully fragrant, *L. odoratus*, Sweet pea; they are also excellent for cut flowers.
This is an annual or perennial plant with bluish-green, angular stems, light, pinnate leaves with supporting leaflets, and papilonaceous flowers with a bell-shaped, five-lobed calyx, five petals, of which the top one is erect (flag), two grow sideways (swords) and two are fused in a boat shape (keel). The seeds grow in pods.
L. latifolius, perennial pea, is a winter-hardy, perennial plant, up to 2.5 m tall. It flowers from June to August (from the second year). The stems have wings and the bluish-green, oval or oblong leaves grow in pairs, winding at the tip. It has clusters of five to fifteen short-stemmed, non-fragrant, pinkish-red flowers, 2.5 cm across. There are several varieties with pink, white, red and purple flowers, such as "Rose Queen", large pink flowers, "White Pearl", white flowers, an easy plant for fences, walls (support with a frame) and pergolas.
Grow in a more or less sunny spot in well-drained, fertile soil. Prune back hard in October/November. Propagate from seed (autumn or spring) and by dividing the plant.
L. odoratus, Sweet pea, is an annual up to 3 m tall, with limp, winged, self-clinging stems, and oblong, oval, pointed leaves with two supporting leaflets, tendrils and long, flowering stems in the leaf axilla, with two to seven fragrant lilac flowers. There are many cultivars in different colours, usually combined and subdivided into varieties with large flowers ("Spencer", "Royal Family"), early flowering varieties ("Spencer Praecox") and low-growing varieties ("Bijoux"). Train along gates, chicken wire or supporting wire in a sunny spot, in well-drained, fertile, moist soil. Because of diseases, regularly plant in different places. Pick flowers frequently to encourage longer flowering. Water during dry periods and feed every

two weeks. Propagate from seed outside in March/April, for early flowering under glass, in February/March.

Lonicera
Honeysuckle

🌿 ↕ 4-10 m ○ ◐ ● ❀ 5/6-7/9 ❀ 7-10 ❄

Lonicera is indigenous in temperate, warm and subtropical regions of the northern hemisphere. It comprises about 200 evergreen and deciduous species of woody-stemmed shrubs and climbers, including L. periclymenum, common honeysuckle, which grows commonly in the woods, brushland and dunes in the Netherlands. A number of climbing species are eminently suitable for growing on fences, walls, trellises, pillars, garden fences and pergolas. This climbing plant has shoots which wind in a clockwise direction, and whorls of smooth-edged leaves with short stems or no stems. The circles of tubular or bell-shaped, orange-white, pink or purple flowers and red berries grow at the end of the stems. L. x brownii "Dropmore Scarlet" is a semi-evergreen plant, 3-5 m tall, which flowers form June to October. It has sturdy stems, bluish-green leaves, and odourless, bright red flowers. Good for planting in the shade. L. caprifolium, garden honeysuckle, is a deciduous plant. It grows 3-6 m tall, flowers from May to June, and has hollow stems, stalkless leaves, and fragrant, pale yellow flowers. It is sensitive to mildew. L. x heckrottii is deciduous. It flowers from June to September and is moderately tall. The leaves are dark green at the tips and bluish-green lower down. It has purple flowers with a light yellow heart, and flowers for a long time; L. x heckrottii "Gold Flame" is orangey-red with a golden yellow heart. L. japonica, Japanese honeysuckle, is semi-evergreen, 4-6 (sometimes 10) m tall and flowers from May to July, with fragrant, trumpet-shaped white flowers, which later turn yellow, and black fruit; L. japonica "Aureoreticulata" is moderately winter-hardy and has yellow-veined, bright green leaves. L. periclymenum, common honeysuckle, is deciduous, grows to a height of 4-7 m, and flowers from June to September, with large clusters of fragrant, yellowish-white or red flowers. It is popular with bumble bees and moths, and has red berries from July to October, which are very popular with birds; "Belgica Select" flowers profusely and has thick, sturdy stems, dark, bluish-green leaves and pale purplish-pink or yellow flowers;

"Graham Thomas" has yellowish-white flowers; "Serotina" has purplish-red with white flowers.
This plant requires a sunny or slightly shady spot, and loose, moist, nutritious soil; older plants become bare at the bottom. Prune back some stems or the entire plant (in spring). Propagate from winter and summer cuttings and from seed (autumn).

Lonicera caprifolium "Inga", Honeysuckle

below: Lonicera etrusca

Malus "Cox's Orange Pippin", Apple

supporting poles and stretched wires. Plant approximately 2-2.5 m apart, tie back the strongest shoots to the left and right, trim the middle shoot and prune the other shoots. Repeat this every year (in early spring). Remove shoots growing forwards and backwards and tie or remove young branches. Pick apples with the whole hand (to prevent bruising). Propagate from cuttings and seed.

Maurandya

· | 1-2 m ○ ❀ 7-10

Maurandya is indigenous in the United States, Mexico and the Caribbean. It is sometimes sold under the name *Asarina*. The remaining plants are not winter-hardy in temperate regions, but when they are cultivated as an annual, with proper support, they will look very attractive against a sunny wall with their beautiful

Malus
Apple

⛰ | 2-2,5 m ⊘ ❀ 4-5

Malus, is indigenous in the temperate regions of Europe, North America and Asia. It provides us with what is undoubtedly the most important fruit, the apple. It is not particularly suitable for being trained against a wall, because it is sensitive to heat, but thrives as a fruiting hedge (like *Cydonia*, the quince).

This shrub or tree has attractive leaves, dark pink buds and white, pink or purple flowers. Depending on the variety, it produces fragrant, light-green, yellow, streaked, brown or dark red (decorative) apples, which ripen earlier or later. Early varieties include *Malus* "James Grieve", a yellow, juicy, tasty dessert apple with red stripes; "Yellow Transparent", yellowish-green, crisp, slightly sour dessert and cooking apple, to be eaten within three days after ripening; summer varieties include "Cox's Orange Pippin", a flattish, round, greenish-yellow, fragrant apple with a red flush; "Jonagold", a large yellow, juicy dessert apple, striped with red; "Elstar", a golden yellow, fragrant, crispy, tasty apple, with a red blush.

It is suitable for west or east-facing walls, in a cool, airy spot in moist (clay) soil, rich in humus, or trained in a hedge with

leaves and splendid flowers.

This herbaceous, climbing plant has winding, climbing stems, spiralling leaf stems, tubular and trumpet-shaped flowers and deeply indented, five-lobed petals.

M. barclaiana syn. *Asarina barclaiana*, 1.5-2 m tall, has attractive, long-stemmed, triangular, pointed lobed leaves, and beautiful, soft-haired, funnel-shaped, purplish-pink, violet or white flowers, 3-7 cm long.

M. erubescens (syn. *Asarina erubescens*) has glandular hairs, red or triangular, coarsely serrated leaves and pink flowers up to 7 cm across.

This plant is suitable for sunny walls and pergolas in well-drained soil, rich in humus. Train young stems and use supports. Propagate from seed in February/March at 20° C. Plant out in April.

Maurandya erubescens

Menispermum
Moonseed

○ ↕ 4-5 m ○ ⊘ !

Menispermum canadense

Menispermum is indigenous in temperate regions in Central and North America, Mexico and eastern Asia. It comprises only three species of spreading, twining plants, which can completely overrun slow-growing shrubs growing nearby. It is a woody-stemmed climber which loses its leaves and forms underground runners. It has attractive, long-stemmed palmate, lobed leaves, and unremarkable loose umbels or panicles of male and female flowers and black fruit.

M. dauricum has hairless young shoots, long, short-lived, non-clinging tendrils (which need to be tied up), and shiny green, heart-shaped, slightly lobed leaves, 6-12 cm long on stems, loose umbels of flowers and black sickle-shaped fruit.

This is an attractive, fast-growing, leafy plant, suitable for quickly covering walls and fences with a wire mesh cover. Grow in a sunny or slightly shady spot in any fertile soil. Prune back to the ground in spring. Propagate from cuttings and seed.

Mina lobata

It comprises about 45 species, of which a number with a strikingly shaped bitter or sweet-tasting fruit are cultivated as a vegetable. In warmer regions they can be grown in any spot, in cooler climates they are cultivated in a heated greenhouse, but can also be grown as an annual in a sheltered, warm spot.

This is an annual or perennial, herbaceous, twining climber, with fast-growing stems, long clinging tendrils, long-stemmed, heart-shaped, deeply lobed leaves, and oblong, smooth or spiny fruit, 10-25 cm long, which tear open when they are ripe, revealing brown, red or white seeds, and red pulp.

M. balsamina, is an annual, with thin, palmate, deeply indented, three to five-lobed leaves, small yellow flowers, and broad, oval, green fruit up to 8 cm long, which turn an orangey-yellow and are covered with wrinkles and warts.

M. charantia, bitter cucumber, is an annual, with long-stemmed, heart-shaped, five to nine-lobed leaves, long-stemmed, fragrant yellow flowers, pendent, greenish-white fruit which later turns orangey-yellow, 20-25 cm long, covered in warts, and with brown or white seeds and bright red pulp.

M. cochinchinensis, the spiny bitter cucumber, is a perennial with dark green, leathery, three to five-lobed leaves and yellow flowers with a black or purple heart, and oval, green, pointed, cone-shaped spiny fruit, which later turns orangey-red and is up to 12 cm long.

Grow against chicken wire or other supporting material in a sunny, warm, sheltered spot in well-drained, fertile soil, e.g., a mixture of leaf mould, clay and manure. Keep moist. Propagate from seed (heated greenhouse, early spring). Plant outside when the chance of night frost is past.

Mina

· ↕ 4 m ○ ✿ 7-9 ⚘

Mina comes from Mexico and comprises only one species, which is sometimes classified under the closely related *Ipomoea* or *Quamoclit* genus.

M. lobata (syn. *Ipomoea lobata, Quamoclit mina*) is a perennial, cultivated as an annual in temperate regions. It is a rampant, twining climber, with stemmed, heart-shaped, pointed, three-lobed leaves (the middle lobe is narrower), branching, slightly pendent flowering stems which grow in the leaf axilla, and clusters of tubular, bright red flowers which turn orangey-yellow or white, with greatly protruding, yellowish-white stamens. Also suitable as cut flowers.

This is an attractive climbing plant. Plant against (south-facing) walls and pergolas in a sunny, sheltered spot, using some support, in well-drained, fertile soil. Propagate from seed in an unheated greenhouse (April). Place in a pot and plant out mid-May.

Momordica

Bitter cucumber

· ○ ↕ 1,5-4 m ✿ 6-8

Momordica is indigenous in tropical and subtropical regions in Asia and Africa.

Morus

Mulberry

⚘ ↕ 3-6 (-10) m ○ ◉ ✿ 5 ✦ 7

Morus is indigenous in tropical and subtropical regions of North and South America and Asia, etc. It comprises 10 varieties, of which *M. alba*, the white mulberry, is cultivated for its leaves, which are fed to silkworms, and *M. nigra*, the black mulberry, has always been grown for its fruit. These two varieties are known all over the world.

This is a woody-stemmed, deciduous tree or shrub which is winter-hardy in a sheltered spot. It buds late (end of May), and has differently shaped, spreading, heart-shaped,

Momordica charantia,
Bitter cucumber

sometimes deeply lobed, roughly serrated
leaves with a (slightly) heart-shaped base,
small, inconspicuous, dioecious, green
flowers, male, ear-shaped catkins, female,
compact, spherical catkins, and edible false
fruit which resemble raspberries or
blackberries and can be eaten fresh or made
into jam, etc.

M. alba, the white mulberry, 6-10 m tall, is
monoecious, with unlobed or irregularly
lobed, coarsely serrated leaves, 6-12 cm
long, which are bright green on the upper
side and slightly hairy on the underside,
turning yellow in autumn, It has stemmed,
flowering catkins and creamy-white fruit,
1-3 cm long.

M. nigra, the black mulberry, is dioecious.
It has coarsely serrated leaves which are
dark green on the upper side and hairy and
light green on the underside. The sweet-sour
fruit is dark red, later turning almost black.
This tree is suitable for training against a
warm, south-facing wall in a sheltered spot
in the sun or semi-shade in lime-rich, moist,
well-drained (sandy) soil. Tie the shoots in a
fan shape from a short trunk, removing the
other shoots and avoiding overcrowding.
The fruit appears mainly on young shoots.
To retain the shape and keep the tree
youthful, remove only the older shoots.
Propagate from seed and by layering.

Morus nigra, Mulberry

43

Pandorea jasminoides
"Variegata"

Pandorea

🌱 ↕ 6 m ○ ✿ 5-8

Pandorea is indigenous in tropical and subtropical regions of Australia etc. It comprises eight species, of which two

are cultivated. They are not winter-hardy and should overwinter in a frost-free spot. This evergreen, twining climber has whorls of unevenly pinnate leaves, and clusters of trumpet-shaped flowers at the end of the stems.

P. jasminoides (syn. *Bignonia jasminoides*), bower vine, has compound, shiny green leaves, consisting of 5-9 oval to lanceolate leaflets and clusters of trumpet-shaped, pink-throated, cream coloured flowers, 5 cm long.

P. pandorana (syn. *Bignonia australis, Tecoma australis*), Wonga-wonga vine, has compound, fern-like, scalloped leaflets and less striking, cream-coloured clusters of small flowers with a violet or pinky-red throat.

For sheltered (balcony) walls; the plant can be used as a tub plant with a supporting frame. From May to October in a sheltered, sunny spot in nutritious, moist soil. Prune after flowering, overwinter in a light, cool place (min 5° C). Propagate from cuttings (heated greenhouse, 20° C), layering (summer) and seed (spring).

Pandorea jasminoides
"Rosea"

Parthenocissus tricuspidata

Parthenocissus

 ⬚ 9-20 m ◯ ⊘ ◉ ❀ 6/7-8 ✳

Parthenocissus is indigenous in America and Asia and comprises 15 species, of which most bear beautiful orange, dark red or purple leaves in the autumn. Eventually these vigorous climbers can completely cover the facade of a house; keep an eye on it because it clings tenaciously to any sort of background (gutters, windows etc.).
This is a deciduous, climbing shrub with tendrils with clinging, sucker-like pads, single or compound palmate serrated leaves, insignificant green flowers and small blue berries which develop only after a hot summer.
P. henryana (syn. *Vitis henryana*) has angular stems, slightly thicker, often white-veined, serrated leaves consisting of five leaflets, and blue berries.
P. quinquefolia (syn. *Ampelopsis hederacea*), Virginia creeper, five-leaved ivy, has yellowish-green stems which later develop aerial roots, sucker-like pads, shiny green, palmate leaves, consisting of 5-7 leaflets

which turn scarlet in autumn, and blue-black berries; *P. quinquefolia* var. *engelmannii* grows vigorously with coarser leaves.
P. tricuspidata has creeping and climbing stems, and thick, heart-shaped leaves with three lobes, consisting of three serrated, shiny green leaflets turning pale yellow and then red, and red and blue berries;
P. tricuspidata "Green Spring" has bright green leaves which turn a reddish purple, 15-20 cm long; "Lowii" has small, lobed leaves consisting of three deeply indented, serrated, bright green to bronze coloured leaflets. Suitable for walls. "Veitchii" has copper-coloured shoots and beautiful orangey-red leaves in autumn; "Veitchii Boskoop" has bronze-coloured stems and young leaves, and older leaves which turn from dark green to brown to scarlet; "Veitchii Robusta" grows very powerfully and has coarser leaves.
This is an extremely fast-growing plant for any sort of wall in the sun or shade, in any nutritious soil. After planting, first prune back hard. Propagate from winter cuttings.

Passiflora foetida,
Passion flower

Passiflora
Passion flower

◯ ↕ 3-9 m ◯ ✿ 5-9 🏺

Passiflora is indigenous in tropical and subtropical regions of America and Asia, and has beautiful symmetrical flowers. There is only one reasonably winter-hardy species.

This is a woody-stemmed climber with spiralling tendrils which develop in the leaf axilla and twine around leaves, branches and stems. The shoots are rigid at first, and later become flexible. The large flowers have five sepals and petals, and a central corona of filaments on a long stem, with five stamens, and above this, the pistil with three styles. They open at different times of day, usually for only one day. The fruits vary greatly in shape and size, and develop only after long, hot summers.

P. coerulea, the blue passion flower, grows 6-9 m tall, and has light green, five to seven-lobed leaves, and slightly fragrant single flowers, 6-10 cm across, with a white or pale pinkish-red crown and a second crown which is blue at the top with a white band below and deep purple at the bottom. The fruits are oval and an orangey-red colour.

Suitable for sunny, warm, south-facing walls, sheltered on a terrace or balcony. Bind up young shoots, keep moist in summer and feed occasionally. In the first few years, cover well in winter and prune back in spring. Propagate by layering root runners and from top cuttings.

Periploca

○ ↕ 9-12 m ○ ✿ 6-8 ❋ !

There is only one species of *Periploca*, which is indigenous in the temperate and dry regions of Africa, Asia and Europe, that is cultivated for the garden. This could be due to the fact that the stems secrete a toxic, milky juice when they are damaged. *P. graeca*, Silk vine, is a woody-stemmed, deciduous, twining plant with hairless, oval to oblong, smooth-edged leaves, 6-10 cm long, which are a shiny dark green on the upper side and pale green on the underside. The long-stemmed umbels of fragrant, star-shaped, yellowish-green flowers, 2.5 cm across, grow in the leaf axilla or at the end of the stems, with a dark purple inside, spotted with white and with a white heart. The brown pods are up to 12 cm long. This plant grows vigorously and is suitable for pergolas, pillars, old trees etc., in a sunny spot in any nutritious, airy soil. Propagate from root cuttings (spring).

Periploca graeca

below: Phaedranthus
buccinatorius

Phaedranthus

🌱 ↕ 5 m ○ ✿ 6-8

Phaedranthus is indigenous in Mexico, and has become widespread in Mediterranean regions. It comprises only one species, *P. buccinatorius*, which is sensitive to frost, and therefore requires at least the protection of a wall or an unheated greenhouse to survive the winter.
P. buccinatorius (syn. *Bignonia cherere*, *Distictis buccinatoria*), Mexican blood flower, is a vigorous, climbing, evergreen shrub, with square stems, pairs of short-stemmed, leathery leaves, fairly long, wiry, branching tendrils and groups of trumpet-shaped, purplish-red flowers with a yellow calyx up to 12 cm long.
In warmer regions it is suitable for covering garden partitions. In temperate regions, plant against sheltered, warm, sunny walls in nutritious soil. Prune back after flowering or in early spring. Remove dead leaves and cover carefully in winter. Propagate from stem cuttings using rooting powder at 18-21° C (spring).

Phaseolus

• ⬆ 4 m ○ ✿ 6-9

Phaseolus is indigenous in tropical regions of Central and South America and southern Asia. It is a well-known vegetable genus, and provides French beans, runner beans, brown and white beans, as well as Lima beans. The pods of *P. coccineus* are also edible beans. This usually annual climber, which twines in an anti-clockwise direction, has leaves consisting of three leaflets which become limp when it grows dark, and white, yellow, red or purple papilionaceous flowers with a crinkly flag (the top petal), in smaller or larger groups, and pods with many seeds, which are usually edible.
P. coccineus (syn. *P. multiflorus*), scarlet runner, is a perennial, cultivated as an annual, with stems 4 m long which twine in an anti-clockwise direction, broad, smooth-edged leaflets, long-stemmed, prolific clusters of large, bright red, purple or white flowers, and rough, green fruits with large coloured or white seeds; "Bicolor" has reddish-white flowers and coloured seeds: "Scharlachrote Riesen" has scarlet flowers; "Albiflora" has white flowers. This is a fast-growing climber which can be trained against fences and trellises, screens, pergolas, loggias, balcony walls etc., in a warm, sunny spot in deep, well-drained, nutritious soil. Keep moist, and remove pods to encourage longer flowering. Remove wilted plants. By means of successive sowings, open spots can be filled up again. Sow in groups of three from the beginning of May; they will germinate after nine days.

Phaseolus coccineus
"Painted Lady"

Pileostegia

⊿ ↕ 7,5-10 m ◉ ❀ 8-10

Pileostegia is indigenous in China, and
comprises three species, one of which is
moderately winter-hardy and can survive
mild winters.
P. viburnoides is a slow-growing, evergreen,
climbing shrub with woody stems, short,
adventitious roots, leathery whorls of oval,
strongly veined, smooth-edged or serrated
leaves up to 18 cm long, and attractive,
creamy-white umbels of small, cup-shaped
flowers with protruding stamens.
This plant is suitable for shady, warm spots
in fertile, well-drained moist soil. Cover
thoroughly in winter. Propagate from
cuttings in summer and seed (spring).

Pileostegia viburnoides

Pisum, Pea

Pisum
Pea

• ↕ 2 m ○ ❀ 6-8

Although *Pisum*, indigenous in Europe and
Asia, is mainly known for the ubiquitous
edible peas of many varieties, it is also an
attractive flowering plant which can
brighten up a fence or partition with the
help of some support.
P. sativum, an annual, has limp stems up to
2 m long, bluish-green compound leaves
consisting of 4-8 oval, oblong,
smooth-edged leaflets with tendrils at the
top, large supporting leaves surrounding the
stem, and clusters of usually two
greenish-white, red, purple or striped,
papilionaceous flowers which grow in the
leaf axilla. It has fairly straight, green or
purple pods.
This is suitable for wire constructions,
trellises etc. in a sunny spot in nutritious,
well-drained soil. Pick young pods
regularly. Propagate from seed (from April).

Prunus domestica,
"Victoria"

Prunus
Apricot, almond, cherry, peach

⚘ ↕ 2-5 m ○ ◑ ✿ 3-4/5

Prunus is indigenous in temperate regions all over the world. It is a large genus comprising 430 species and countless (cultivated) varieties. A number of species are valuable for their fruit (plums, cherries, almonds, peaches and apricots) and for their ornamental value. There is an enormous variety available; several can be trained in a fan shape against a south-facing wall, or cultivated as a fruiting hedge.

This evergreen or deciduous, woody-stemmed tree or shrub has spreading, stemmed, serrated leaves, dioecious white, pink, or sometimes yellow flowers, and usually edible fruit with stones and flesh, which grow singly, in small groups, in umbels, clusters or bunches.

P. armenica, the apricot, is deciduous and sensitive to frost. It flowers in March to April before the leaves develop, with short-stemmed, white or pale pink, single flowers, and has pale yellow to orange, velvety, hairy fruit. Eat fresh, does not keep long. Suitable for training against a south-facing wall in a sunny spot, protected from rain. It requires loose, nutritious, slightly moist soil. Old branches and shoots should be pruned after harvesting.

P. cerasus, the Morello cherry, is deciduous

right:
Prunus armenica, Apricot

and winter-hardy. It flowers in April to May, has fairly strong, hairless leaves, and bright white or pinky-red umbels of flowers with one or more green leaves at the base. The flattened, round, sour fruit is a red to dark red colour. Only eat when completely ripe. It can also be used to make juice, jam etc. "Morel", the Morello cherry, has slender branches, long-stemmed flowers, and dark red, extremely sour fruit. "Rhexii", the ornamental cherry, flowers later with long-stemmed, double white flowers, 3 cm across. They are suitable for training against a wall (in a fan shape), or growing in a fruiting hedge in the sun or semi-shade, in any cold soil that is not too heavy. After the harvest, prune back fruit-bearing branches to the young shoots.

P. domestica, the plum or damson, is deciduous and winter-hardy. It flowers from March to April. The branches are hairy at first, and are later bare, reddish and shiny. The leaves are up to 10 cm long, with soft hair on the underside. It has greenish-white flowers and bluish-black, later sometimes yellow or orange, sweet, fragrant fruit, 4-10 cm long; "Reine Claude Verte" has

small, round, green or yellow juicy fruit which is ripe at the end of August; "Victoria" has large, round to oblong red fruit which is ripe in mid-August; because of its broad crown it is not suitable as a fruiting hedge. It requires a warm, sunny spot and nutritious, moist soil, rich in humus and not too acid. Thin out after flowering.

P. dulcis (syn. *P. amygdalus*), the almond, is deciduous and fairly winter-hardy.

It flowers in March to April before the oblong, pointed leaves appear on the young green branches. It has white to pinkish-red flowers and felted, hairy fruit which spring open when ripe (in September). It is suitable for training against a warm, south-facing wall (in a fan shape), in a sunny, sheltered spot in loose, nutritious soil; the fruit appears on one-year-old shoots; prune back the older shoots. The honey glands on the leaf stems attract ants and wasps.

P. persica, the peach, is deciduous and sensitive to frost. It flowers from March to May and has smooth, bare, sometimes angular branches. The unstemmed, white or dark pink flowers appear before the leaves develop, and the round, juicy, fragrant, slightly hairy,

reddish-yellow fruit, 7-12 cm across, develop singly or in twos; the nectarine, a relation of the peach, has a shiny, smooth skin; eat fresh, does not keep long. It is suitable for training against a south-facing wall (loosely trained or fan shape), in a sheltered, warm spot, in loose, nutritious soil. The flowers attract bees and flies. Propagate from seed, by layering and from cuttings.

Prunus cerasus, Morello

Prunus dulcis, Almond

Pueraria lobata

Pyracantha
Firethorn

⚘ ↕ 1-6 m ○ ◉ ❀ 5-6 ❀ 9-12

Pyracantha is indigenous in southeast Europe and the Near East. It comprises about 15 species, several of which are winter-hardy; they are vigorous, trailing plants which flower profusely, produce large numbers of berries and can be used for covering walls. A process of selection has produced a variety which is resistant to scab, an unpleasant disease which used to affect nearly all species.
Generally this is an evergreen shrub of medium height, though it is much taller as a trained plant. It has shiny, dark green leaves, numerous compact white or yellow clusters of flowers, and many red, orange or yellow berries.
P. coccinea is an evergreen, winter-hardy species, 1-2 m tall, which can be trained to

Pueraria

○ ↕ 3-6 m ○ ❀ 7-9

Pueraria is indigenous in southeast Asia etc. and comprises about 35 species, of which only one, *P. lobata*, is cultivated. Using supports it is a good climber for covering walls, but can also be used as ground cover to cover large areas.
This deciduous, twining climber has thick, woody roots and woody, winding stems, large, usually lobed leaves, and clusters of blue, purple or white, papilionaceous flowers growing in the leaf axilla. In a western climate the pods rarely develop.
P. lobata (syn. *P. hirsuta*, *P. thunbergiana*), Kudzu vine, is a sprawling climber with large, tuberous roots, slender, hairy stems which grow to a length of 5-6 m in cultivation, and hairy, broad, oval, slightly-lobed leaves consisting of three leaflets. It has fragrant, compact clusters of bluish-purple or purple flowers and narrow, hairy pods.
This plant is suitable for a sunny (south-facing) wall in well-drained, nutritious soil. Train carefully and prune regularly. The parts above the ground die off in winter. Cover in winter and it will develop again in spring. It is resistant to drought. Propagate by removing underground runners, from seed and from cuttings (spring).

right:
Pyracantha coccinea
"Orange glow",
Firethorn

a height of approximately 5 m, with many stiff, thorny stems, leathery, shiny green, oval or oblong leaves, double yellow or white clusters of flowers, and small, bright red, scarlet, orange or yellow berries; the cultivars and hybrids which are cultivated are mainly those which are resistant to scab, including "Golden Charmer", a spreading, branching variety with many orangey-yellow berries; "Mohave", a large, broad variety with bright red berries, less winter- hardy; "Orange Charmer", dark orange berries; "Orange Glow", dark orange and dark red berries; "Red Column" is more erect, with bright red berries; "Soleil d'Or", a broad, bushy variety with yellow berries. This strong, trained plant looks attractive against a yellow or red brick wall. Plant in a sunny or slightly shady spot in nutritious, well-drained soil. Improve the soil if necessary. Bind up branches and prune flat. Propagate from summer and winter cuttings.

Pyrus communis, Pear

Pyrus
Pear

 2,5-12 m 3-4

Pyrus is indigenous in warm and tropical regions of Europe, western Asia and North Africa. It comprises about 30 species, of which *P. communis* is an important source of pears for consumption. Varieties which like warmth are extremely suitable for training against a wall or as a fruiting hedge.

P. communis, the common pear, is a deciduous, woody-stemmed, often thorny shrub or tree, with oblong to oval, finely serrated leaves on stems, pure white flowerheads consisting of eight to nine flowers with red, and later yellow anthers, and round to narrow, oblong, hard or soft fruit, which ripen at different times, depending on the variety. Pears suitable for training include "Bonne Louise", delicious dessert pears, which ripen in September/October; "Doyenné du Comice", large, broad, irregularly formed, green to yellowish-brown, sweet, juicy dessert pears; "Rode Williams", reddish-green dessert pears; "Triomphe de Vienne", very large, regularly formed, green to bronze, juicy, dessert pears.

It is suitable for training against a warm, south-facing wall, in a sunny spot, in airy, nutritious, well-drained (clay) soil. Prune back regularly. Propagate from seed and cuttings. The flowers attract bees, flies and moths.

53

Quamoclit x multifida

Quamoclit pennata

Quamoclit

⊡ [!] 1,5-6 m ◯ ❀ 7-9

Quamoclit is indigenous in tropical regions of America. It is not always classified as a separate genus, and is sometimes classified with *Ipomoea*.
This is an annual or perennial, herbaceous, twining plant, with long, limp stems, single, divided or lobed leaves, and clusters of red or yellow trumpet-shaped flowers which grow in the leaf axilla and have a long, tubular corolla, spreading petals and protruding stamens.
Q. coccinea (syn. *Ipomoea coccinea*), Red morning glory, is an annual 3-4 m tall, with heart-shaped, smooth-edged leaves, sometimes angular at the base, and scarlet, orange or ochre clusters of fragrant, long-stemmed flowers, 2 cm across.
Q. pennata (syn. *Ipomoea quamoclit*), Cypress vine, is an annual, 6-7 m tall, with finely divided leaves, and scarlet flowers, 3-5 cm long, with star-shaped spreading petals. This fast-growing plant flowers profusely and is suitable for fences, pergolas etc. Bind up stems carefully, plant in a sunny spot in nutritious soil. Propagate from seed (outside from May).

54

*Rhodochiton
atrosanguineus*

Rhodochiton

· ↕ 2,5 m ○ ✿ 7-9

Rhodochiton comprises only one species, the perennial *R. atrosanguineus*, indigenous in Mexico, which flowers profusely with striking flowers; it can easily be cultivated as an annual.

R. atrosanguineus (syn. *R. volubile*, *Lophospermum atrosanguineus*) grows up to 2.5 m tall, and has limp stems, flexible, winding tendrils, heart-shaped, pointed, serrated, light green to reddish leaves, and characteristic, pendent red flowers on long, thin, pink stems; a narrow, tubular, purple-black corolla, 2.5 cm long, ending in a trumpet shape with five spreading lobes, protrudes from each large, bell-shaped, pinkish-red calyx.

This plant is suitable for growing on sheltered, warm (balcony) walls, along fences and trellises and other supports, in a sunny spot in fertile, well-drained soil. Water regularly and add (cow) manure if necessary; the plant will not survive the winter outside, but it is fairly easy to grow new plants from seed in spring. Propagate from seed in the greenhouse at 15-20° C (February/March).

*Rhodochiton
atrosanguineus*

Rosa "Paul's Scarlet climber", Climbing rose

Rosa x borboniana "Zéphyrine Drouhin", Climbing rose

Rosa
Climbing rose

🌱 ↕ 2,5-6 m ◯ ◉ ✿ 6-9

Rosa is indigenous in temperate regions of the northern hemisphere. It is an extremely popular garden shrub, and is cultivated in many ways. A process of cross-fertilization and selection has produced a large variety of climbing, or rather trained roses, with stems more than 3 m long, which can be trained in different ways, on pergolas, wire fences, walls and gates.

Long-flowering climbing roses were originally tall shrubs with very long shoots, usually compound leaves and beautiful single or double, often fragrant flowers which grow singly or in clusters, generally throughout the season; these shrubs are trained broadly (to encourage profuse flowering) against posts, walls or the side walls of a rose bower. They generally remain too low for pergolas or gates (3 m).

Prune once a year in spring. Bind up main stems as horizontally as possible. After two or three years, prune lateral stems almost down to the main stem. This means they will form new flowering stems.

Occasionally allow shoots to grow in order to replace older main stems. Deadhead roses to encourage flowering.

Climbing roses which do not flower continuously, flower on stems the second year. Therefore the young shoots are not pruned. The long, limp stems are suitable for pergolas and rose arches; the main stems should be bound together every week from the beginning for support, the flowering shoots are pruned back in the following spring, and the old main stems are cut away down to the ground, and possibly replaced. Tie back using string or copper wire and tubing.

Long-flowering, climbing roses include *Rosa* "Blaze", 2.5-3 m tall, with large, leathery green leaves, and large pink clusters of fragrant, semi-double flowers; "Breath of life", up to 2.5 m tall, slightly fragrant, fully double, dark, old rose flowers; "Clair Matin", 2-3 m tall, not very fragrant, whitish-pink or pink flowers, also suitable for a north-facing wall; "Compassion", up to 3 m tall, beautifully fragrant, double pink

Rosa "Pierre de Rousard"

Rosa "American Pillar"

flowers; "Zéphyrine Drouhin", 4-5 m tall, no thorns, fragrant, double, pinkish-red flowers, also suitable for a north-facing wall.

Climbing roses which do not flower continuously include *Rosa* "Alchymist", up to 4 m tall, bronze leaves, pleasantly fragrant, double, pale yellow and pink flowers; "Alexander Girault", 5-6 m tall, large, double, dark red flowers which smell of apples; "Dorothy Perkins", 3-5 m tall, double, pink flowers, also suitable for a north-facing wall; "Easlea's Golden Rambler", 4-5 m tall, shiny green leaves, fragrant, double, whitish-yellow flowers; "Elegance", 5-6 m tall, not very fragrant, double, whitish-yellow flowers; "Emily Gray", 506 m tall, shiny, young reddish leaves, large bright yellow flowers; "Excelsa", 3-4 m tall, shiny green leaves, double bright red flowers; "Guinée", up to 5 m tall, beautifully fragrant, double, very dark red flowers, some late flowers; "Lawrence Johnston", up to 10 m tall, large, very fragrant, single, pale yellow flowers, flowers again after an interval, following the main flowering; "Leontine Gervais", 5-7 m tall, large, double, pale, yellowish-pink flowers which smell of apples; "Madame Caroline Testout", 5-6 m tall, not very fragrant, fully double pink flowers, single late flowers; "Maigold", up to 6 m tall,

Rosa "Decline"

flowers; "Coral Dawn", up to 3 m tall, large, not very fragrant, beautiful pink flowers; "Danse des Sylphes", up to 4 m tall, not very fragrant, double, bright red flowers; "Danse du Feu", up to 4 m tall, abundant, dark, scarlet or violet flowers, not very fragrant, suitable for north-facing wall; "Dreaming Spires", up to 4 m tall, slightly fragrant, double yellow flowers; "Etoile de Hollande", up to 4 m tall, very fragrant red flowers; "Flammentanz", 4-5 m tall, light green leaves, double, bright red flowers; "Galway Bay", up to 3 m tall, not very fragrant, double, pinkish-red flowers; "Golden Showers", up to 3 m tall, slightly fragrant, bright yellow flowers, also suitable for a north facing wall; "Händel", up to 4 m tall, not very fragrant, splendid, double, white and pink flowers; "Iceberg", up to 4 m tall, not very fragrant, double, beautiful snow-white flowers; "New Dawn", up to 3 m tall, slightly fragrant, semi-double, whitish-pink flowers, also suitable for a north-facing wall; "Park director Riggers", 3-4 m tall, fragrant, blood-red flowers, also suitable for a north-facing wall; "Swan Lake", 2-3 m tall, large, not very fragrant, double white flowers; "Sympathie", up to 4 m tall, not very fragrant, double bright red

right:
Rosa hybriden +
Hydrangea macrophylla
hybrid

beautifully fragrant, double golden yellow flowers; "Masquerade", up to 4 m tall, not very fragrant, two coloured, yellowish-red flowers, some late flowers; "Meg", up to 4 m tall, slightly fragrant, pale old pink flowers; "Paul's Scarlet Climber", up to 3 m tall, semi-double, splendid scarlet flowers; "Sutter's Gold", up to 4 m tall, fragrant, golden-yellow, slightly red-veined flowers; "White Dorothy Perkins", 3-4 m tall, double, creamy flowers.

If possible, plant in Autumn (October/November) in a sunny spot about 1.5-4 m apart, 20 cm away from the wall. Trim the plant and build a mound of earth around the main stem. Fill the resulting hollows with manure. These plants require well-drained, nutritious soil, rich in humus and with some lime. Dig over to a depth of 60-80 cm, mix in manure. If necessary, improve clay or sandy soil. Prune back in spring and add manure. In general, leave the propagation of these selections to cultivators.

Rosa "New Dawn"

Rosa "Edith de Martinelli"

Schisandra sphaerandra

Schisandra

🌿 ↕ 4-9 m ⊘ ❀ 5-6 ❁ 6-8

Schisandra is mainly indigenous in tropical and subtropical regions of Asia. It comprises about 25 species, some of which are cultivated and are suitable for north-facing walls. The plants are dioecious; the berries, which contribute to its ornamental value, appear only when the female flowers have been fertilized. For proper fertilization, male and female specimens should be grown together.

This evergreen or deciduous climber is sometimes winter-hardy. It has winding, woody stems, long-stemmed, smooth-edged or serrated leaves in groups or spread out, red or orange dish-shaped flowers in clusters or spikes, and purple or scarlet fruit.

S. chinensis is winter-hardy and deciduous. It grows 6-9 m tall and has hairless, reddish shoots, broad, oval, shiny green serrated leaves which are sea-green underneath, creamy or pale pink fragrant flowers, 1-2 cm across, and purple berries.

S. glaucescens is winter-hardy and deciduous.

Schisandra rubriflora

It grows 6 m tall, and has thin, oval, light green, slightly serrated leaves, bluish-green underneath, orange flowers and scarlet berries. *S. rubriflora* (syn. *S. chinensis*, var. *rubriflora*, *S. grandiflora* var. *rubriflora*), is moderately winter-hardy and deciduous. It grows 4-8 m tall, and has leathery, broad, oval, green serrated leaves which are pale green underneath, dark red flowers, 2.5 across, and red berries in drooping clusters.
Grow in a light spot or semi-shade against a (north-facing) wall, out of full sunlight, in nutritious, well-drained, acid soil, poor in lime and slightly moist. Keep moist and water liberally during dry periods. Feed in spring (March/April). Bind up young shoots. Prune in January/February. Cover less winter-hardy varieties in winter. Propagate from seed (winter, in an unheated greenhouse), by layering (September), and from cuttings (July/August as 15-19° C). Overwinter in an unheated greenhouse. The plant does not like being moved.

Schizophragma

⊠ ↕ 6-10 m ⬦ ❀ 7-8

Schizophragma is indigenous in the Himalayas and eastern Asia, and comprises eight species, of which two are cultivated. This is a deciduous climber with adventitious roots, whorls of smooth-edged or serrated leaves, flowerheads with small, white or creamy fertile flowers inside, consisting of four to five sepals and petals, surrounded by infertile flowers consisting of a single large, white, long-stemmed sepal.
S. hydrangeoides, Japanese hydrangea vine, is winter-hardy and grows up to 10 m tall. It has heart-shaped to oval, bright green, coarsely serrated leaves up to 15 cm long, and flowerheads 20-25 cm across, consisting of white fertile flowers and infertile flowers with a white petal, 3-4 cm across; in *S. hydrangeoides* "Roseum", these petals have a pink glow.
S. integrifolium is moderately winter-hardy, up to 6 m tall, with occasionally hairy, dark green, smooth-edged or serrated leaves, pale green on the underside, up to 20 cm long, and white umbels up to 30 cm across.
This plant is suitable for walls, rocks, trees etc. (not for wooden fences) in the semi-shade. It requires nutritious, moist soil, rich in humus, particularly around the roots.

Plant in spring. Prune back to 15 cm above the ground (only the roots of new shoots cling). At first, tie up the plant. In the first few years it grows slowly, with few flowers, but it makes up for this later. In spring, apply a layer of organic material, and water liberally during dry periods.
S. integrifolium should be covered in winter (straw mat) when there is frost. It can be pruned into shape in spring. Propagate from cuttings (July/August) and by layering (October).

Schizophragma hydrangeoides

climbing shrub, tolerates light frost and grows 3-4 (-10) m tall. It flowers from June to September, has long, limp, herbaceous stems, shiny green, oval, smooth-edged leaves up to 12.5 cm long, fragrant, compact umbels of purplish-pink flowers, and sometimes yellowish-white berries; *S. crispum* "Glasnevin" tolerates slight frost and flowers longer and more profusely with dark pink flowers.

S. jasminoides, potato vine, is an evergreen climbing shrub which is not winter-hardy. It flowers from February to November, grows up to 5 m tall, and has long, limp, fast-growing stems, shiny green, oval leaves, 3-5.5 cm long, on stems, and umbels of star-shaped flowers, 1.5-2.5 cm across, which are pale violet, and later turn white; *S. jasminoides* "Album" flowers with flat umbels of white flowers.

S. wendlandii is an evergreen which is not winter-hardy. It flowers from July to September, has prickly stems, pinnate, prickly leaves, and beautiful clusters of lilac flowers, 6 cm across. To keep its leaves in winter, the temperature must be 10-15° C. For sunny to slightly shady, sheltered spots, it can be kept outside against a wall in very mild winters. Grow in nutritious soil with supports such as bamboo sticks, wire,

Solanum wendlandii, Nightshade

Solanum
Nightshade

🌿 ↕ 3-4 m ◯ ◐ ✿ 2-11/6-9 ❗

Solanum comprises 1700 species, and is one of the largest genuses of plants. They are found all over the world, particularly in the warmer regions of America. In addition to well-known vegetables (potato, tomato, aubergine) and exotic fruit (pepino), the genus includes a number of decorative plants, of which some form long shoots and can climb if they are supported. In general, they are not winter-hardy and must be moved indoors in winter in temperate regions, after being pruned in autumn. The indigenous species, *S. dulcamara*, bittersweet, a twining plant for wild gardens, with small, dark purple flowers, is winter-hardy.

This is an annual, biennial or perennial, herbaceous plant, often with spiny stems and spreading, single or double, smooth-edged or deeply indented leaves, star-shaped or bell-shaped, with white, violet or dark purple flowers which grow singly or in clusters, and have yellow, protruding, cone-shaped stamens in the middle, surrounding the protruding white style, and berries which are often poisonous.

S. crispum, a bushy, semi-evergreen,

trellises etc. for climbing. Water liberally during the growing season and feed every two weeks. Prune in spring or autumn. The plant can be placed inside for the winter in a cool spot from November to May, after being pruned.

Propagate from top cuttings (summer at 20-25° C) and by layering.

Stauntonia

🌿 ↕ 10-12 m ○ ◍ ❀ 3-4

Stauntonia is indigenous in eastern Asia. It comprises about 15 species, one of which is moderately winter-hardy, and can even be used to brighten up a north-facing wall with some winter cover.

This is an evergreen, woody-stemmed, twining climber with compound leaves, fragrant clusters of male and female flowers growing in the leaf axilla. They are bell-shaped and white or yellow with purple stripes, consisting of two groups of three petals; the outer ones are slightly broader.

Stauntonia hexaphylla

Berries develop only in warm climates. *S. hexaphylla*, 10-12 m tall, has hairless stems, compound leaves consisting of 3-7 leathery, oblong, oval leaves on stems, fragrant, slightly drooping white or yellow flowers on stems, with purple stripes inside, and purplish, edible, sweet berries, 2-5 cm across.

This is an attractive, easy plant to grow; it requires some support for climbing. It can be planted against a (north-facing) wall in a sunny or slightly shady spot, in any fertile soil. Feed occasionally during the growing season. Prune back if necessary in the spring. Protect against frost. Propagate from seed and cuttings (spring).

left:
Solanum jasminoides, Nightshade

Tamus communis

Tamus

⬚○⬚ ⬚↕⬚ 1,5-2,5 m ⬚○⬚ ⬚❀⬚ ⬚!⬚

Tamus is indigenous in Western Europe, from Great Britain to the Mediterranean, on the Canary Islands and Madeira.
It comprises five species, one of which has spread as far as Belgium, where it is found in beech woods and hedgerows.
This is a perennial, herbaceous, twining climber, dioecious, with greasy, tuberous roots. The stems can intertwine, and it has spreading, heart-shaped, sometimes three-lobed pointed leaves, and flowerheads consisting of many small green flowers in the leaf axilla. It has red berries; the roots and berries are often poisonous.
T. communis is deciduous, 1.5-2.5 m tall.
It has black, greasy, poisonous roots, triangular to heart-shaped, light green leaves which turn purple and bright yellow in autumn, single, long clusters of green,

star-shaped or bell-shaped flowers and attractive, juicy, green or red poisonous berries. Grow out of the reach of children, against a trellis, in a sunny or slightly shady spot, in fertile, moist soil. It can be pruned back in spring. Propagate from seed (April, *in situ*), and by dividing the roots (spring).

Thladiantha

○ ↕ 1,5-10 m ○ ✿ 6-7

Thladiantha is indigenous in Asia and comprises about 15 species, two of which are cultivated. They are not very well known dioecious climbers.

This perennial herbaceous climber has tendrils, tuberous roots, hairy or hairless, heart-shaped or oval, pointed, serrated leaves, large, golden-yellow, bell-shaped flowers with a five-lobed calyx and five folded-back petals - the male flowers usually grow in groups, the female flowers singly in the leaf axilla - and oblong, scarlet, fleshy fruit, striped along the length.

T. dubia, is a winter-hardy plant with hairy stems up to 1.5 m long, light green, coarse-haired, heart-shaped to oval, pointed, serrated leaves, 7-10 cm long, clusters of male flowers, 5-8 cm across, female flowers, 5 cm across, on hairy stems, and coarse-haired fruits with black seeds.

T. oliveri is moderately winter-hardy, and grows vigorously. It has hairless stems up to 10 m long, larger leaves up to 20 cm long, and it flowers more profusely.

Because of the rapidly expanding system of roots, it is suitable as a specimen plant against fences, gates and bowers, with a slightly rough background for the tendrils to attach themselves. It requires a sunny spot in any fertile soil. Prune back in autumn. *T. oliveri* should be covered in winter. Propagate from seed and by dividing the plant (spring).

Thladiantha dubia

*Thunbergia grandiflora
"Alba"*

Thunbergia

· ↕ 1,5-6 m ○ ⊛ 6-9

Although *Thunbergia*, which is indigenous in tropical and subtropical regions of Africa and Asia, is mainly sold as a house plant, a number of species can be cultivated outside as annuals, covering large parts of a (south-facing) wall in a short time, if trained on supports.

This annual or perennial, woody-stemmed or herbaceous climber has whorls of smooth-edged or serrated leaves, attractive, often single, blue, yellow, orange or white flowers, consisting of a large, trumpet-shaped, spreading corona with five parts, and a dark or light-coloured heart.
T. alata, Black-eyed Susan, grows up to 1.5 m tall, with heart-shaped or saggitate, serrated leaves, winged stems, and bright orange flowers with a black eye, growing in the leaf axilla. Overwinter if possible at 5-10° C, and prune back in spring.
T. erecta flowers profusely and has thin stems, thin, oval or oblong leaves, and dark, purplish-blue flowers with a long, whitish-yellow corolla and a yellow heart.
T. grandiflora, blue trumpet vine, has woody stems, oval, coarsely serrated leaves up to 20 cm long, and pendent clusters of large blue flowers.
This is an easy plant to grow in a sunny, warm, sheltered spot in nutritious soil. Plant out seedlings when there is no danger of night frost. Use support, such as wire mesh etc. The plant dies down in winter.
Propagate from seed (at 20° C) and from cuttings (spring).

Thunbergia alata

Trachelospermum

🌱 ↕ 2-6 m ○ ❁ 5-6

Trachelospermum (syn. *Rhyncospermum*) is indigenous in tropical and subtropical regions of eastern Asia and North America. It comprises 30 species which are not winter-hardy and of which *T. jasminoides*, Star jasmine, can tolerate some frost after being hardened off. It can remain outside in mild winters, though other species should be brought inside for the winter at 4-10° C. This evergreen, twining, climbing shrub has stems containing a milky juice, oblong to oval, smooth-edged leaves, and white, yellowish or violet umbels of flowers with a long corolla and spreading petals.
T. asiaticum (syn. *T. divaricatum*), is not winter-hardy, up to 6 m tall, and has leathery leaves, 3-6 cm long, and umbels of terminal, snow-white flowers.
T. jasminoides is moderately winter-hardy, 2-5 m tall, with slender stems which twine around supports, and shiny, dark green, broad to lanceolate leaves, 5-10 cm long. The beautifully fragrant, loose umbels of white, star-shaped flowers, grow on stems in the leaf axilla.
This climber grows slowly in the first few years against a fence or trellis, in a sheltered, sunny spot in nutritious soil, rich in humus. Protect against frost in winter or move the plant indoors. Prune back the plant if it grows too tall. Propagate from cuttings in summer.

Trachelospermum jasminoides

Trachelospermum asiaticum "Tricolor"

Tropaeolum majus, Nasturtium

Tropaeolum peregrinum, Canary creeper

Tropaeolum
Nasturtium

• ↓ (0,2) 0,5-3 m ○ ◐ ❀ 6-10 ⚒

Tropaeolum is indigenous in the mountains of South America. It comprises about 90 species, including annual and perennial species, some which form tubers and some climbing plants. The leaves (of all the species) contain compounds of mustard oils. They have a sharp taste and are sometimes eaten in salads. They are also very popular with cabbage white caterpillars.
This herbaceous, juicy climber clings to the background with the long leaf stalks attached to the middle of the spreading leaves, which are shield-shaped and sometimes lobed. The single, long-stemmed, symmetrical flowers consist of five sepals, one of which has a long spur which secretes nectar, and five petals, narrower at the base. It has schizocarps. *T. majus*, garden nasturtium, is a perennial plant, cultivated as an annual. It has hairless, round to kidney-shaped, greyish-green, slightly wavy leaves with blunt corners, and a yellow calyx with pale yellow, orange or red petals which are fringed at the base; the unripe fruit can be conserved in vinegar and used instead of capers. The countless cultivars are mainly cultivated as annuals, including low-growing, compact varieties (*T. majus* var. *nanum*) and twining climbers up to 2.5 m tall, with single or double flowers in every shade of yellow, orange, red, pink or salmon, with dark, golden, coloured and wavy leaves; the seeds are sold by colour, though usually combined.
T. peregrinum (syn. *T. canariense*), Canary creeper, is an annual climber, 2-3 (-5) m tall, with strongly indented leaves consisting of 5-7 leaflets and pleasantly fragrant, yellow flowers, with green, hooked, curved spurs, and finely divided, fringed petals.
T. tuberosum is a perennial climber, 2-3 m tall, with yellow, red-streaked tubers, reddish, fast-growing shoots, shield-shaped or palmate, five-lobed, blunt leaves, red flowers and bright blue berries. The tubers are eaten (rather like potatoes). This plant tolerates some shade and grows up against canes, shrubs, hedges etc.
Suitable for growing against trees, walls, fences, trellises etc. The soil should not be too heavy and clayey; this encourages leaf growth but not flowers. Sow annuals *in situ* from May (for earlier flowering, sow under glass in April and plant out mid-May). The tubers should be lifted immediately when the flowers die down, and be stored for the winter in moist peat in a cool place. Plant out again in nutritious or poor, dry

soil in May. Flowering stems will keep for ten days in a vase as the flowers gradually open. Sensitive to black aphids. Propagate from seed. Nasturtiums will self-seed.

Vitis
Vine

⚘ ↕ 7-10 m ◯ ◐ ✿ 5-7 ✾ 6-10

Vitis is found all over the world in temperate and hot regions. It is particularly well known for *V. vinifera*, the grape vine, which produces grapes for making wine. Viniculture takes place in warm regions in southern Europe, South Africa, North and South America etc.; in colder regions they are grown in greenhouses. A number of the 60 to 70 species are very suitable as decorative plants because of their beautiful leaves and splendid autumn colours.
This vigorous, deciduous climber was originally dioecious. It has woody, branching stems and single, palmate, indented leaves, inconspicuous, androgynous flowers in cultivars, and berry-like fruits.
V. amurensis, amur grape, is winter-hardy, 6(-12) m tall, with palmate, three to five-lobed, finely serrated leaves with a heart-shaped base, which turn a beautiful crimson or purplishred in autumn, and black, slightly sour grapes.
V. coignetiae, Crimson glory vine, is a good, winter-hardy climber up to 25 m tall, with large, wrinkled, bright green leaves, which turn yellow, yellowish green, reddish or crimson in autumn and have brownish-red hair underneath. The panicles of flowers are 10-15 cm long, and it has narrow bunches of unpalatable black fruits.
V. vinifera, grape vine, up to 7 m tall, has large, lobed light green leaves which turn a beautiful colour in autumn, and blue or black fruit. *V. vinifera* "Boskoop's Glorie" has delicious blue grapes; "Incana" has downy-white, hairy leaves which turn red in autumn and black grapes; "Purpurea" has dark red and purplish-green leaves turning purple, and black grapes; "Vroege van der Laan" has delicious white grapes.
Vitis "Brant" is the most winter-hardy variety, with green, red-veined leaves which

turn red, and green-veined, small back, sweet grapes.
This plant is suitable for training against (south-facing) walls, fences, horizontal trellises, pergolas. or trees, in a sunny or slightly shady spot, in normal, nutritious soil. The flowers appear on the laterals of the previous year's shoots. Prune these shoots down to three eyes in December. Propagate by layering and from eye cuttings (winter).

Vitis vinifera, Vine

Vitis coignetiae, Vine

Wisteria sinensis

Wisteria floribunda

Wisteria

🌿 ↕ 8-10 m ○ ◑ ✿ 4/5-7

Wisteria is indigenous in North America and eastern Asia. It comprises 9-10 species of attractively flowering, twining climbers which can grow many metres tall with stems twining in a clockwise or anticlockwise direction round trees or other supports. This deciduous, woody-stemmed, climbing shrub is winter-hardy, and can develop fairly thick trunks. It grows in May/June and has spreading, pinnate leaves with an odd number of up to 19 leaflets, beautiful, drooping racemes of blue, pink or white, short-stemmed, papilionaceous flowers, and pods.

W. floribunda, Japanese wisteria, 8-10 m tall (up to 20 m tall when growing in the wild), with a trunk up to 2 m tall, stems which twine in a clockwise direction, compound leaves up to 40 cm long, consisting of 11-19 oblong, pointed leaflets, and racemes 15-30 (-60) cm long of large, fragrant, pale violet flowers, 2-2.5 cm long. When mature, it flowers profusely against a warm (south-facing) wall; W. floribunda "Alba" has racemes, 30-40 cm long, of white or very pale purple flowers; "Longissima Alba" has racemes, 60-70 cm long, of white flowers; "Macrobotrys", has racemes, 50 to 150 cm long, of whitish-violet flowers; "Rosea" has racemes up to 45 cm long, of pale pink flowers; "Violacea Plena" has double violet flowers.

W. x formosa (a cross of W. floribunda and W. sinensis) has compound leaves consisting of 9-15 large leaflets, and racemes, 25 cm long, of pale purple flowers. All the flowers open at the same time; W. x formosa "Issai" has racemes 30 cm long of light and dark pinkish-violet flowers.

W. sinensis, Chinese wisteria, 30-40 m tall, has stems twining in an anti-clockwise direction, compound leaves up to 35 cm long, consisting of 7-13 leaflets, and very fragrant racemes, 16-30 cm long, of lilac-blue flowers. It flowers profusely from April to May, and often again, slightly less profusely, in July/August. W. sinensis "Alba", has white flowers; "Black Dragon", dark purple, double flowers; "Caroline" flowers profusely for a long time, with very fragrant, double, deep violet flowers; at the end of the summer, prune back that year's shoots to 5 cm; grow in sun and semi-shade.

W. venusta, Silky wisteria, up to 10 m tall. The stems wind in an anti-clockwise direction. It has velvety, hairy leaves and broad racemes, 10-15 cm long, of fragrant, creamy-white flowers, 2-3 cm across, which open at the same time.

*Wisteria floribunda
"Macrobotrys"*

This plant is suitable for sturdy pergolas, bowers, (south-facing) walls with trellises or wire supports. When it is trained, keep an eye on the growth. It should not be too close to the wall (leaves at the back fall off for want of fresh air). Plant the root clump in a sunny spot in deep, well-drained, nutritious, lime-rich soil. Prune in June/July and at the end of the winter. Propagate by layering.

Lists of climbing and trailing plants

See descriptions for specific varieties and other information.

Self-clinging climbers

	Height (m)	Flowering period
Ampelopsis	6 -10	Jul-Aug
Bryonia	- 4	Jun-Aug
Campsis	3 -10	May/Jul-Sep
Decumaria	-10	May-Jun
Eccremocarpus	2 - 3	Jun-Oct
Euonymus	0,5- 3	Jun-Jul
Hedera	6 -20	Sep-Oct
Hydrangea	5 -20	Jun-Jul
Parthenocissus	9 -20	Jun/Jul-Aug
Phaedranthus	- 5	Jun-Aug
Pileostegia	7,5-10	Aug-Oct
Schizophragma	6 -10	Jul-Aug
Thladiantha	1,5-10	Jun-Jul

Climbers requiring support

	Height (m)	Flowering period
Akebia	6 -10	Apr-Jun
Aristolochia	5 -10	May-Jul
Basella	- 6	May-Jun
Calystegia	1 - 5	Jun-Sep
Celastrus	7 -12	Aug-Nov
Clematis	2 -10	Apr/May-Oct
Cobaea	3 - 6	Jun/Jul-Sep
Codonopsis	0,5- 1,8	Jun-Jul
Fallopia	10 -15	Jul-Oct
Humulus	1 - 6	Jul-Aug
Ipomoea	2 - 4	Jul-Oct
Jasminum	2,5- 6	Dec-Mar/Jul-Sep
Lathyrus	0,5- 3	Jun-Oct
Lonicera	4 -10	May/Jun-Jul/Sep
Maurandya	1 - 2	Jul-Oct
Menispermum	4 - 5	Grown for foliage
Mina	- 4	Jul-Sep
Momordica	1,5- 4	Jun-Aug
Pandorea	- 6	May-Aug
Passiflora	3 - 9	May-Sep
Periploca	9 -12	Jun-Aug
Phaseolus	- 4	Jun-Sep
Pisum	- 2	Jun-Aug
Pueraria	3 - 6	Jul-Sep
Quamoclit	1,5- 6	Jul-Sep
Rhodochiton	- 2,5	Jul-Sep
Schisandra	4 - 9	May-Jun
Solanum	3 - 4	Feb-Nov/Jun-Sep
Stauntonia	10 -12	Mar-Apr
Tamus	1,5- 2,5	Aug-Nov
Thunbergia	1,5- 6	Jun-Sep
Trachelospermum	2 - 6	May-Jun
Tropaeolum	0,2- 3	Jun-Oct
Vitis	7 -10	May-Jul
Wisteria	8 -10	Apr/May-Jul

Full sun:

Basella	Periploca
Calystegia	Phaedranthus
Clianthus	Phaseolus
Cobaea	Pisum
Cucurbita	Pueraria
Eccremocarpus	Pyrus
Ficus	Quamoclit
Ipomoea	Rhodochiton
Maurandya	Tamus
Mina	Thladiantha
Momordica	Thunbergia
Pandorea	Trachelospermum
Passiflora	

Full sun or semi-shade:

Actinidia	Jasminum
Akebia	Lathyrus
Ampelopsis	Lonicera
Aristolochia	Menispermum
Bryonia	Morus
Campsis	Parthenocissus
Celastrus	Prunus
Chaenomeles	Pyracantha
Clematis	Rosa
Codonopsis	Solanum
Cydonia	Stauntonia
Decumaria	Tropaeolum
Euonymus	Vitis
Fallopia	Wisteria
Humulus	

Semi-shade or shade:

Decumaria	Parthenocissus
Hedera	Pileostegia
Hydrangea	Schisandra
Lonicera	Schizophragma
Malus	

Fast-growing annual climbers:

Basella	Momordica
Cobaea	Phaseolus
Cucurbita	Pisum
Eccremocarpus	Quamoclit
Humulus	Rhodochiton
Ipomoea	Thunbergia
Maurandya	Tropaeolum
Mina	

Trailing plants: F = edible fruit	Height (m)	Flowering period
Actinidia (F)	6 -12	Jun-Jul
Chaenomeles (F)	1 - 2,5	Mar-May/Jun
Clianthus	1,8- 3	May-Aug
Cucurbita	2 - 6	Jun-Sep
Cydonia (F)	1,5- 3	May-Jun
Ficus (F)	- 4	Jul-Aug
Malus (F)	2 - 2,5	Apr-May
Morus (F)	3 -10	May
Prunus (F)	2 - 5	Mar-Apr/May
Pyracantha	1 - 6	May-Jun
Pyrus (F)	2,5-12	Mar-Apr
Rosa	2,5- 6	Jun-Sep

Campsis grandiflora

Planting

A number of climbers are naturally woodland or forest plants, and are therefore quite happy with a certain amount of shade. This means they are very versatile in the garden. Many grow very easily, but require some kind of support such as a trellis, fence, pergola or arbour, old tree or tree stump. Climbing foliage plants, particularly evergreen ones, can be used as a background for perennials and deciduous shrubs. And some plants, such as *Hedera* and *Hydrangea*, will grow horizontally without being supported and can be used as ground cover.

Some climbing plants make excellent cut flowers; these include *Clematis, Hydrangea, Jasminum* and *Rosa*. Rambling roses grow very vigorously, with long, flexible stems and large amounts of foliage; these are less well suited to very small gardens, but with a little pruning can look superb grown up a tree or used to cover an unattractive shed or fence.

A number of annual climbers are also suitable for covering surfaces quickly.

Never fix trellis straight to a wall: always leave a gap of a couple of centimetres, and remember that the structure will be visible if you use plants which lose their leaves in winter.

Always dig the uprights well into the soil, 50-60 cm deep, as mature plants can be very heavy, particularly when it rains.

Most trailingplants require a great deal of careful pruning and need to be tied in. The loose shape is created by tying two shoots to the trellis and cutting off the centre shoot 50 cm above it. The two strongest of the resulting shoots are then tied in on either side and all others are removed. In the spring, the middle shoot is pruned again and the new shoots are tied in, and so on. Always remove branches growing forwards or too close together.

A hedge can be created using stakes with wire stretched tautly between them, 50 cm apart and up to about 2 m high. Place the stems next to the stakes and train the young shoots horizontally where possible, in July or August. Remove any straggly or forward-growing branches.

Various ready made climbing supports are available in the shops. Lattice work can also be made using impregnated slats.

By means of screws secure together at right angles, or diagonally, 50 cm apart. Secure to the wall using small, 2 cm-thick blocks (for air circulation).

A free-standing screen (trellis) must have a strong foundation: posts should be dug in at least 60 cm deep. The distance between the posts depends on the height and the width of the fence (max. 6 m). A fully covered screen bears a considerable plant weight.

Low brick walls with anchored constructions can also be used.

74

Maintenance

A garden containing a lot of climbing and trailingplants requires rather more work to keep neat. Some plants are self-clinging; others have tendrils or twining leaf stalks, and others still must be tied in if they are to grow in the required form. Tie in plants with string, raffia or special tape, and do not tie them too tightly, or you will constrict their growth.

Before planting, the soil will need to be prepared to suit the needs of the plant. Dig a good-sized hole and work in some well-rotted farmyard manure and, if necessary, lime. Plunge the root ball in water before planting. Dry, sandy soil will hold water much better if you work in some organic material such as compost or garden peat; the compost will also provide additional nutrients. The structure of heavy soils such as clay can be improved by adding sand, compost or peat. Once you have planted the plant, any extra nutrients should just be sprinkled on the surface of the soil. Bear in mind the sizes of the plants: the stated height and spread may not be achieved for years, or even decades.

Normally, early-flowering plants should be pruned after they have flowered, and later ones in the early spring. Remove dead and frost-damaged parts of the plant, and any branches which have not grown in the right direction - in many cases, these can be used as cuttings for propagation.

Dead-heading will often encourage repeat flowering, but in this case the plant is unlikely to bear fruit. You may need to obtain specialist advice on pruning fruit bushes and trees. There is no need to have a major clean-up in the autumn: simply leave the dead leaves where they fall and sprinkle compost over them. This will give a much more natural appearance, and also protect the plants against frost.

Propagation

Some plants can be grown from seed, though this does not apply to cultured varieties which are the result of selection or crossing, or grafted forms. Grafting is best left to the experts, but propagation by layering and cuttings can often be relatively easy.

Layering involves burying a flexible stem in the soil about 15 cm from the tip. Roots form on the buried part, and the tip can then be trained upwards. Once the stem has rooted, usually after about a year, it can be separated from the parent and grown as a new plant.

Cuttings involve removing part of the plant and using it to grow a new one. Autumn, or hardwood cuttings involve removing a woody part about 15 cm long in late autumn and planting it in sand in a frost-free place. Roots will form after the winter, and the cuttings can then be potted up and eventually grown outdoors.

Summer, or semi-ripe cuttings are the tips of young shoots which have not yet turned woody. These should be taken from June onwards, with the cut made just underneath a bud, dipped in rooting powder and then potted up.

Other kinds of cutting include stem tip cuttings, using the tip of a stem and some leaves; leaf-bud cuttings, consisting of a short piece of stem with a leaf and leaf-bud, and heel cuttings, where a "heel" of old wood is peeled away from the parent plant.

Trained fruit trees
Plant the support poles no more than 5 m apart and up to 60 cm deep, then stretch taut wires 50 cm apart up to a workable height (approx. 2 m) between the poles.
After planting, bend one strong shoot to the left and one to the right, and cut back the middle stem; during July and August of the subsequent years, tie on the two strongest laterals left and right, cut back the middle stem, and remove all other shoots. Once the middle stem has reached the top wire, secure and bend it over. Remove any stems that are growing away from the main shape.

Small workers in the garden

Nocturnal life around climbing twiners

Climbing and twining plants turn bare walls, fences and pergolas into green structures in which birds can nest close at hand. Many of these climbing twiners flower with beautiful, scented flowers. A good example is the honeysuckle, a true night-flowering plant. The flowers open only in the late summer afternoon or in the early evening, emitting an overwhelming sweet fragrance. It soon attracts the first moths such as the hawk-moth.

Hawk-moths

These moths fly only at dusk and at night, and they certainly can fly ! They are sturdy creatures with strong flying muscles which enable them to perform acrobatic tricks. They do not even take the trouble to settle on a flower, but feed on the nectar while they hang in the air with rapid movements of the wings, just like hummingbirds. They drink with their tongue, which is several centimetres long, and during the rest of the day it is curled up, under the head, like the spring of a watch. They certainly eat their fill from honeysuckle, which contains exceptionally large amounts of nectar. The tubular flowers are often more than half full. Hawk-moths need a lot of food - their reckless style of flying consumes enormous amounts of energy. The speed at which they fly is easily visible when they circle around an outside light, attracted by the brightness and the scent of flowers, which is increased by the heat of the lamp. This also reveals that there are many different species of moths in all sorts of sizes, shapes and colours. However, the hawk-moth, which derives its name from its markings, is the best known. Hawk-moths - as well as all other moths - constitute the main part of bats' daily diet.

Common pipistrelle,
Pipistrellus pipistrellus

Bats

There are far more of these mysteriously perfect nocturnal predators than one would think. There are many different species, some of which are very rare, while others are widespread. By day, they hide in caves, hollow trees, the cracks of walls, nesting boxes, church towers or lofts. It is only in the evening that they fly out, making sounds which are inaudible to us and which are bounced back to their own ears like a sort of echo when they strike an object. In this way bats not only manage to avoid obstacles, but are also able to find their prey, and this is how moths are snatched out of the air in a fraction of a second.

Hawk-moth,
Agrius convolvuli

Bats themselves have very few natural enemies. For example, they are far too fast for owls - the only birds of prey which hunt at night. Owls are restricted to mice and sleeping birds. In fact what applies to bats also applies to owls; there are far more than we suspect. There are tawny owls and long-eared owls even in towns, in parks and large gardens, and with a bit of luck, a hollow tree in a garden in the suburbs could house a beautiful little owl.

List of symbols

- ⊡ annual
- ⊡⊡ biennial
- ◻ perennial
- ◻ bulbous plant
- ◻ tuberous plant
- ◻ tree
- ◻ shrub
- ↕ height in cm
- ↔ interval between plants in cm
- ○ full sunlight
- ◐ semi-shade
- ● shade
- ❀ flowering months
- ✳ winter-hardy
- ! poisonous
- ✂ suitable for cut flowers
- ⚬ berry
- ⌸ keep moist at all times, compost should not dry out
- ⌸ keep moderately moist, compost may dry out slightly
- ⌸ keep fairly dry, only water during growing period
- ⌁ spray, avoid spraying when plant is flowering